PROLIFIC POETRY:

Views from the mind of Esham Abdul Giles presented in artistic form

ESHAM ABDUL GILES

PROLIFIC POETRY

WRIITTEN BY ESHAM ABDUL GILES

EDITED BY KALENAH WITCHER

Cover Design by BAJA UKWELI

For further information about this book, write all inquires and permissions to;

Focus Write Inspire LLC.

PO BOX 373

NEWARK, NJ 07101

www.FocusWriteInspire.com

Library of Congress Cataloging-in-Publication Data is available.

Library of Congress Control Number: 2012941455

ISBN-13: 978-0-615-63728-0

esham abdul giles

DEDICATION

Bismillah ir rahman ir rahim

In loving memory of my great grandmother, C. Elizabeth Boss, my grandmother, Lois Porter, my uncle, Fredrick Porter, aunts Vivian Porter, Rose Mary Boss, Vanessa Burns and my beloved family and friends who have passed.

This book is dedicated to my Mother and Father, "Thank you for bringing me into this world…without you none of this would even be possible." To my children, siblings, Rasheed, Muhammad, Vince and Latisha, To my grandparents Grandpop and Grandma Giles, To the mothers of my children, "Thank you for the beautiful blessings we share…Our Children." Extended family and friends, "You inspire me to do great things…I couldn't imagine life without you." Ibn and Mequa, We can accomplish anything, if we have faith, focus and work hard. Thank you ALL for your love and support. I LOVE YOU dearly, may GOD protect and bless us.

Esham

"You were born with wings, why prefer to crawl through life?"

Rumi

PROLIFIC POETRY

ESHAM ABDUL GILES

TABLE of CONTENTS

Chapter One: Tributes

Chapter Two: Tribulations

Chapter Three: Influence and Injustice

Chapter Four: Consequences

Chapter Five: Desires, Discernment, Discipline

Chapter Six: Ego, Strength, and Power

Chapter Seven: Knowledge of Self

Chapter Eight: Clear Signs and Relief

PREFACE

Who am I? I am someone who has mastered the art of exploring self. I know I am here to serve a high purpose and with this gift from GOD I will do so. To master self and get to know who you truly are deep down to your core you must take some you time. Pray, meditate, reflect...Delve deep into your inner spirit…find that free access point. You're only remembered or as good as the last thing you do in this world we live in, that's just the way it is. But remember this as you soul search and find your inner spirit, "everything in life happens for a reason…whether good or bad, it's a lesson for us to learn and grow." The ones that can bounce back from any adversity thrown at them are the ones who will never be defeated. If you're going thru trials, tribulations or unexpected change you must learn to face them and put things behind you that are out of your control…Rise to challenge any situation, show the world how you will respond, because they're watching and if you let doubt, fear discouragement over throw you then they will know what you're about. But if you comeback from anything thrown at you; the brink of defeat then the world will know just what your made of…Trust in yourself, your inner strength, your inner spirit, your purpose. Everything within me points to higher purpose; understanding, acceptance, patience, enlightened to what is real and why I am here. Many people will go a lifetime without knowing their purpose and why they're here. They just go on existing…Don't fall into this sink hole. At a point in my life I was lost; I fed my ego and not my soul. I gave into temptation and Shaitan instead of GOD and righteousness, until he found and saved me from self destruction and self torment. One thing we must learn in life is that, "we can't fool the soul." You can pretend every day, but the only one who will be fooled and suffering is you… Think more of yourself than that which surrounds you and comforts you with temporary relief from facing your unhappy soul. We all serve a purpose in life; so dig deep and find your higher purpose. All my experiences, from the lows to the highs have helped me grow to be the man that I am today. God willing, I will continue to grow and evolve. In this book, *Prolific Poetry*, I will share my purpose, my wisdom, my passion with you.

Esham

Acknowledgements

Serron Green and BaJa Ukweli for designing the cover.
Rochelle Petty of DreamStarr Publishing for all your insight and knowledge.
Dr. Kalenah Witcher for editing support.

Thank you to all my friends from Ivy Hill and the entire Vailsburg section, Myrtle Avenue, Irvington, cities and towns near and far as well as my coworkers over the years: NJMVC, NJDCA, FED EX, BOMBARDIER, NIKE.

Much respect to the entrepreneurs in my life including; Chris B, Pete Burke, Razor Sharp Barbers, A. Tim Jewell, Elite Cuts, Syl, the Barber, Drastic Entertainment, Mission Entertainment, Race Entertainment, Eric Graham, Souls of Helen Halal Foods, Risque Entertainment, Lisa Ford, Tax Professional.

Special acknowledgements to Senator Ronald Rice, for believing in me and granting me opportunity. Much love to West Ward Councilman Ron Rice,Jr…and the entire City of Newark Council. Family and friends employed by the City of Newark and the County of Essex. Sincere thanks to my friends of the Newark, Irvington and East Orange Police Departments.

Lifelong gratitude for the Irvington, Roselle, Linden, Newark, and Seton Hall libraries. Let's maintain access to free books!

So, O Man, prayer is essential for the perfection of the praise of GOD— to which you are bound as much as the rest of creation. Like the birds, then you will rise away from the earth and soar to the skies — resulting in your transformation from a worldly to a heavenly creature.

Qur'an, Surah An Noor 24:41

"And Allah is Knower of what they do."

Indeed I have fallen; May Allah grant me redemption.

EAG

INTRODUCTION

The reality of our existence includes our experiences of happy and sad times, suffering, death, birth and renewal. I don't live my life in a passive state; some situations have greatly affected and molded me. When some are distressed the presence of friends or the comfort in material objects gives them a feeling of what I call "temporary happiness". In my mind, the best way to deal with any stress is to seek prayer and solitude even if for a day or two to process and plan moving forward with life.

My form of dealing is writing. Writing allows me to calm and control my mind with my pen…to release all from within. We all are more than capable to push through anything if we truly believe we can. I have no doubt that releasing my art in a positive way will have significant impact on someone who wants to express similar feelings.

This book, *PROLIFIC POETRY* deals exclusively with my reality. My writing identifies many inner dark feelings and negative states of mind like anger, hatred, frustration, betrayal, foolishness and pride and also acknowledges love, compassion, happiness, tolerance, acceptance, contentment and remembrance. *PROLIFIC POETRY* is a collection of musings from the mind of a thoughtful writer and feeler seeking therapeutic release. Some are funny while others are sad. Some are insightful and uplifting. Some are encouraging; others are nostalgic.

My hope is that this book will absorb, touch your inner spirit and will serve as a guide of inspiration, reflection and confirmation that no one person is alone in this world. Moving from one story to the next, you the reader may be able to define some of your realities through my experiences or you just may have a different or understanding entirely.

PROLIFIC POETRY is an honest book, a book of familiarity, feelings and experiences. There will be no persuading or preaching here. The intention is to communicate wisdom, comfort and hope. This work taps into some of everything I feel and or have been through. Life is not all dark. I have dreams to be more and so long as I have faith, passion, perseverance and patience I can achieve, "PROLIFIC POETRY."

"Don't be satisfied with the stories that come before you…unfold your own myth."

Rumi

Chapter One: Tributes

pro·lif·ic [pruh-lif-ik]
adjective
Producing in large quantities or with great frequency; highly productive: *a prolific writer.*

PROLIFIC

Create a phenomenon,
Discover what is real
The world will know the potential and things I feel,
ESHAM ABDUL GILES!
I'm committed to win;
Bring out my favorite pen,
Words appear on paper
Let the process begin
To achieve great success is the meaning in the end!
So, explore the pages of my Greatness,
They will show that I'm creative and artistic,
Dynamic, great work, simply PROLIFIC!
Believe what I say, "Anything in this world CAN be won."
By a mind that is fully committed,
KNOWING what it takes to get things done!
Skeptics and Underestimating haters hold no weight here,
Strong WILLED; No FEAR.
Become your number 1,
Maximize the LIFE GOD placed upon thee,
Strong hold your dreams with authority.
Take your time, do things to PERFECTION,
Let nothing stop what is DESTINED.
I take full advantage of my position,
Humble and gratefully I share my vision,
Showing the world why I AM PROLIFIC.

esham abdul giles

par·a·mount

[**par**-*uh*-mount]
adjective

1. chief in importance or impact; supreme; preeminent: *a point of paramount significance.*

2. above others in rank or authority: superior in power or jurisdiction.

esham abdul giles

3

PARAMOUNT

Legends, Icons, Ghetto Celebs,
I carry more than status or washed up street legacy.

You guys are PATHETIC to believe you move KINGS.
Where is the wisdom from your conglomerate of failure?
Street Kings with big names, lifelong jailers.

Things change by the minute,
Never mind daily,
How will you contribute to this forever evolving society?

Miss me with war stories and what you used to be, or how you held it down in jail.
Not interested in limited convo of how you learned to perfect drug deals.
Explain to the young ones, "When you're in there's a struggle to get out."
Learning from your past,
Now that's PARAMOUNT.

Politician and Preachers with so called big names
Deceiving liars, sellers of false promise don't fool me,
Prey on the naive and the weak with words of deliverance and change,
Smile, smut and coach them to believe,
Back room deals, lobbying with drug dealers, hidden babies,
Gift of gab, "you're the crime scene."

Brothers of the dark Mosque,
Cultivate,
Not cult and mate,
Persuading women they are less than,
Is not ISLAMIC!

No cameras, grandstanding, yelling and screams,
Tell the public what you really care about Legal pimps?
MONEY!
All you fools claim to be leaders of the people,
NEWARK will wake up and discover your truth.
The only one you're concerned about is YOU.

esham abdul giles

4

No admiration, adoring or special privilege,
You're just a man to me if anything, "The Devils Weapon."

Controversy?
"NO!''
Truth is told!
Never afraid to speak or get things out,
My criminal buddies,

I am PARAMOUNT!

esham abdul giles

Dreaming of a destiny that's meant for me.

EAG

esham abdul giles

DREAMER

My vision, my art, and the picture I paint for me,
What does it all mean?
Am I realizing my dreams?

Let the writing begin,
I have to win
Maybe there is one out here who wants to listen.

Remove all doubt,
Conquer my fear,
Heart beats harder as Dreams are near.

This works for me,
This is my music; the pen is my instrument,
Dreaming of one out here who wants to listen.

Speak and write with passion,
Dreams come true,
You believe in YOU!

Sun rise; sunset
Plus or minus
I won't regret,
Awake the darkness; Grab the light
ULTIMATE!

Appreciate the accomplished,
The Dream is realized and to be cherished.

esham abdul giles

LOIS CLEMENTINE BOSS-PORTER

[1]eter·nal
adj \i-ˈtər-nᵊl\
Definition of ETERNAL
a : having infinite duration : everlasting <eternal damnation> b : of or relating to
eternity c : characterized by abiding fellowship with God <good teacher, what
must I do to inherit eternal life? — Mark 10:17(Revised Standard Version)>
a : continued without intermission : perpetual <an eternal flame> b : seemingly
endless <eternal delays>
: valid or existing at all times : timeless <eternal verities>

esham abdul giles

My Eternal love For My Grandmother

I love you Nanny. This is for you.

As my mother and father came to a split,
I thought all things came to an end.
Then there was my grandmother to take us right in.
You were the soul, heart, and rock of the family,
Allah only knows how much I miss my Nanny.

We often had chores, I thought they were strict
And if we gave you a problem you made us get that switch,
It had to be tough Nanny being a grand to six.
You often sat down to tell me how important school was,
I miss you saying it's time for the family reunion.
When Sundays come you would make a big dinner,
We sat at the table sometimes to find sautéed liver,
Oh my! That stuff made me shiver.
You would say, "eat your food and don't hesitate,
You're not going any place until you clean that plate."
After I ate I would run for cover,
My oh my how I miss you grandmother.

When my mother would chastise, I thought she was being mean,
You were always there to give me a shoulder to lean.
You told me, "Esham, I may not agree with her methods,
Don't be upset it's for your protection."

esham abdul giles

9

As the years would pass, family ups and downs,
You would be there to turn things around.

Then the day came and you got sick,
The Alzheimer's was quick to set in,
As memory loss was taking effect,
I hated to see you like that.
Kim stepped up to relieve you of the pain,
She was your guardian angel and
I know you are now the same.

Although you have been called to the Heavens
Allah said it was time to go,
I know you're walking in fields of gold.
We love you and you'll always be missed,
I speak for all the family when I say this,
"Our love for you is eternal Grandmother."

esham abdul giles

10

And We have enjoined upon man, to his parents, good treatment. His mother carried him with hardship and gave birth to him with hardship, and his gestation and weaning period is thirty months. [He grows] until, when he reaches maturity and reaches [the age of] forty years, he says, "My Lord, enable me to be grateful for Your favor which You have bestowed upon me and upon my parents and to work righteousness of which You will approve and make righteous for me my offspring. Indeed, I have repented to You, and, indeed, I am one of the Muslims.

Qur'an, Sura al-Ahqaf 46:15

esham abdul giles

UMI

The foundation of our lives,
The reason we are here,
Thank you dearly for everything.
Every day is your day,
We know how hard you worked for us to be great.
You are unmatched.
Your love we greatly appreciate.
Although you try hard, you can't protect us from everything
You are not to blame; these are Allah's life lessons.
You give us your all, over and over.

The foundation of our lives,
The reason we are here,
We thank you for everything,
Your sacrifice we greatly appreciate.
Our permanent rose.
Your love continuously shows and grows,
The definition of strength and what it means to be strong,
You're more than an UMI (mother) to us;
Our angel a reflection from Allah's kingdom,
Love that knows no boundaries.
Wanting nothing more for us but to be our greatest and to succeed.
The gift of life is what you gave us,
As we are all now grown men,
The testament to this is, "We always will be your children."

The foundation of our lives,
The reason we are here,
We thank you for everything,
Our shining star we greatly appreciate.

esham abdul giles

Listen, my son, to your father's instruction and do not forsake your mother's teaching.

Proverbs 1.8

esham abdul giles

My Son, My One and Only Son

My prayers were answered my son, my one and only. They laid you in my arms and I knew right away that the love I have for you would be wonderful and beyond compare. Though your mother and I didn't always agree, the love we share for you should be never doubted. We love you unconditionally, my son, my one and only son...

The years they flew by, I watched you grow from a little man, to a man strong and tall you became the man of whom I am proud. As you begin your adult life, this opens new chapters in both our lives especially for you my son, my one and only son...

I know I didn't always do the right thing and was not always good at mentoring as I was young and growing myself, I knew that I could never go back and fix all the wrongs so I work very hard to set a new track record my son, my one and only son...

We have been through so much over the years: anger, joy and so many tears. There is not a day that goes by that I don't think about you. As you work toward your goals I will always support you. Even though I may not agree with all of your decisions and choices, I'll be your steady advocate and coach. Now you're a man and on your own path. I pray you become prosperous and more successful than your Dad. I love you and now you know how I feel when I look at you my son, my one and only son.

esham abdul giles

14

Destiny 9/4

She will be my little girl for the rest of my life.

EAG

esham abdul giles

Destiny 9/4

On September 4th the greatest gift I could ask for,
You are destiny; my rising star.
Nothing motivates me or inspires me more,
It's you I live for,
My pride and joy
Destiny 9/4.
My focus is for you,
My inspiration is from you,
My love, heart and soul are you,
My job is to protect you,
For all of your life I'll be by your side,
The days you cry,
The days you smile,
From the first steps you took,
until now in your high school books,
The proud dad I am as I smile and look,
My princess has grown,
I will guide you forever with love, realness and tenderness,
Preparing you everyday to understand how you are to be treated.
I love you.
My day is now your day,
Destined to be born 9/4,
My greatest gift,
Nothing greater I could ask for,
My beautiful, lovely daughter.

esham abdul giles

Terron MEEK covin
1972-2011

might·y (mite)
adjective.
might·i·er, **might·i·est**
1. Having or showing great power, skill, strength, or force: *MEEK!*
2. Imposing or awesome in size, degree, or extent: **MEEK!**
3. Great in amount, or importance; exceptional: *MIGHTY MEEK!*

esham abdul giles

Mighty MEEK

MEEK!
I wonder why,
As days go by
I look at your pictures,
And ask why?
This wasn't supposed to be the outcome of your LIFE!
Mighty MEEK!
The father,
The son,
The brother,
The dear friend,
You live on and will never be forgotten.
This by far is not the end of your journey,
ALLAH has plans for you in eternity.
Loyal Son, Father, Brother and Friend,
I know you're watching over and protecting your Mom and Children.
Words can't express your loyalty and commitment,
When I expressed about the book slightly hesitant,
You said, "Put it out E and don't look back!"
And that's what I'll do, represent the crew.
Reminiscing with Mont, Kadeem, JB and Tuna,
The Block, the Parties, the Weddings,
Everyday seeing you
Talking about our children growing,
So many memories to laugh, cry, and say DAMN about
True to yourself and those you cared for,
Hold no punches, give it to you raw,
One word, PURE!
This I know for sure,
They never wanted to hear your ROAR,
Our brother the LION of M.A.P (MYRTLE AVENUE POSSE)
We love miss and will always represent you MIGHTY MEEK!

esham abdul giles

For my Sisters and Brothers in blood and in spirit. We dreamed, we played, we grew together our way. I never thought that I'd be writing this for you today. IVY HILL.

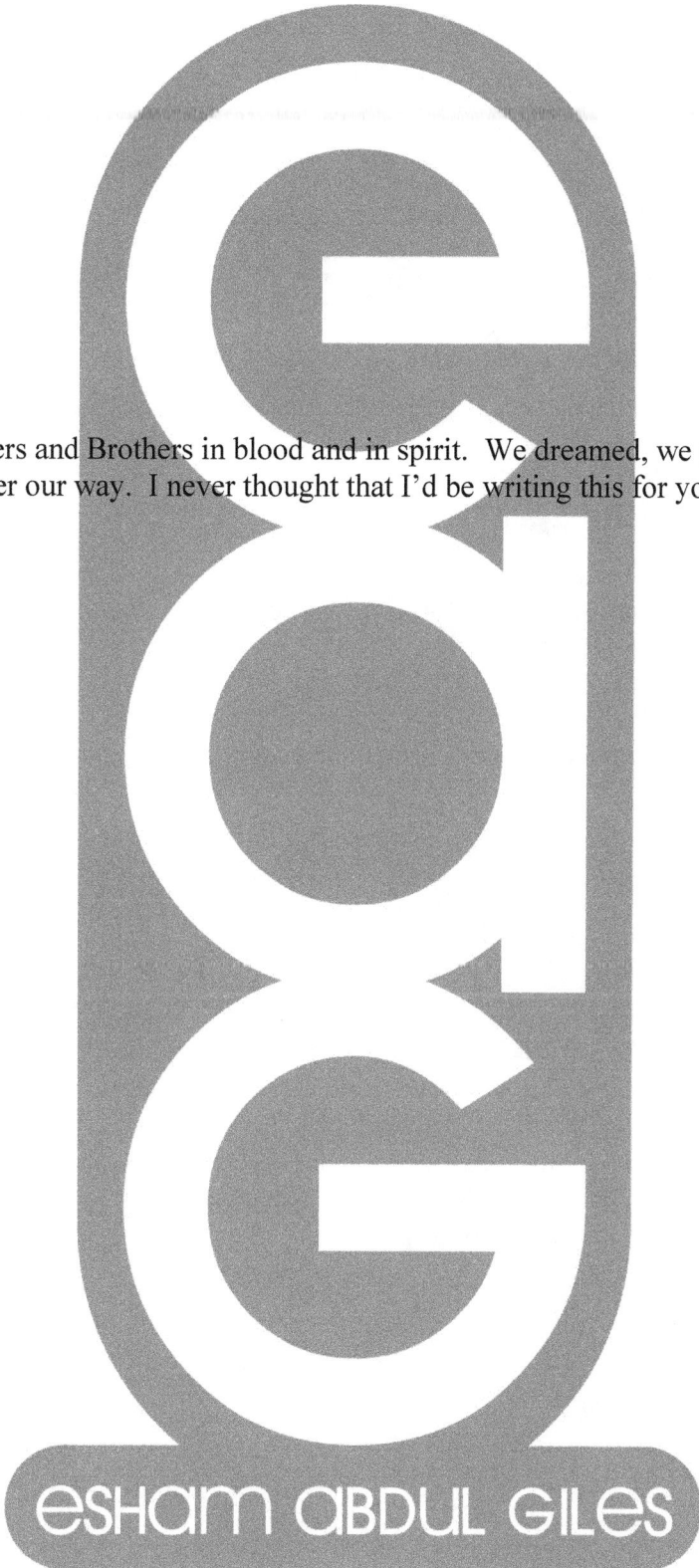

esham abdul giles

IVY HILL

As I stand in the shower, the water hits my back,
I can't help but feel like I'm under attack.
Please let this water rinse away my struggle,
Thinking life is nothing but a puzzle,
Full of turns and many mazes,
How can I forget everything that's ever made me?

There is a dark cloud blanketed on Ivy Hill
I don't want to become a product of these streets,
I've out grown this life style I must bow out gracefully,
I represent all the brothers who are trying to survive,
Can you see the ambition and passion in my eyes?
Ivy Hill is our home to live, not die.

Tired of all the thieving and deceiving,
the back stabbing and envious creep,
These people who know nothing about loyalty.
Stay home, rebuild tradition.
The Hill is the place that I'm missing,
And the days when nothing was fatuous,
So I change my direction to accomplish the mission,
I hear my brothers who have passed on whispering
Esham, slow down, life is real. As I wonder is there
really a curse on all of the boys from Ivy Hill?

As the dark clouds are blanketed over this hill.
These words are forever memorized, I often think
of you Marque and why they left you paralyzed.
You are my brother and our bond is pure,
If only I had the science and money to get you cured.

esham abdul giles

Should I pack up and leave?

What a heavy burden to balance like managing 50 pounds of bricks in wet tearing paper bags!
This wasn't the life we all planned; at times I'm so damn mad.
I need this weight released up off my back.

James tells me, "We're going to live our dreams!"
As I often cried for my man, disheartened
his wish was never seen.

I hear Jerome saying, "Esham, we all we got!"
My brother your words leave my stomach in a constant knot.

Darren says "Esham, bring me your ear, brother we aren't going
nowhere…we survive, but it's now your job to keep Ivy Hill alive."

IVY HILL this is my dedication to you…never forgotten here or not I love all of you

esham abdul giles

The boy forgives so the grown man can move on.

EAG

esHam aBDuL GiLes

FATHER E

Father E, that's the name they gave me,
Let me share how this came to be,
My Uncle Fred said to me, "Esham, your Father's out."
"You're the man of the house now."
"Do you hear me?"
"Take this seriously."
"Yes," I naively offered to Uncle Freddy.

As the oldest of three,
A nine year old is placed with a major responsibility.

I can do this; make things right,
Keep family and values tight.
No laughter, No playing, always a keen eye,
Protecting my brothers is my life.
Young boy; old soul,
Never do I hold resent the life placed upon me.

My cousin Brian would dub me this nickname, "Esh, this would fit you perfectly.
FATHER E!"

And that's what they called me.
I cherish that name and I'm very proud,
As I am the oldest brother of three.
I know many understand this man-child responsibility.

esham abdul giles

23

Blessed is a man who perseveres under trial; for once he has been approved, he will receive the crown of life which the Lord has promised to those who love him.

JAMES 1:12

Su·per·man

[**soo**-per-man]

A person of extraordinary strength.

Supreme discipline; Strong willed

One who prevails by any amount of circumstances thrown at him.

esham abdul giles

I am SUPERMAN

From where it all began to where I am,
Purpose and destiny lay in GOD'S hands,
My path has been long and at times tiring,
But from nothing to something
I am

SUPERMAN.

Love me or hate me I'm destined for greatness,
Impressionistic, evocative, poignant,
A name of meaning; a gift into the light,
Servant of GOD; The good one takes flight.
There are things I can do that nobody else can,
I am called on to RISE and accept the challenge.

SUPERMAN.

My Grandfather said I would be,
More than just an average human being.
As he stated,
"They will try to destroy your name,
Belittle and degraded,
For rise and fame,
But you will overcome all these things."

SUPERMAN.

I have loved; I have lost,
Echoes in eternity keep me to carry on,
A burning flame never to yield,
My journey is inevitable,
I am made of steel,
Very strong minded; very strong willed.

esham abdul giles

SUPERMAN.

Visionary, influential; put here to inspire,
Voice of reason,
The helping hand for you to reach high.
There's no lock that can't be broken,
Release what's inside.
Become a beacon of light; fly high.

SUPERMAN.

As life moves on; I move with it,
My struggle; my strength; release inner spirit.
I am the man of steel.
Again, as life moves on; I move on with it.
Never suppressing the people; genuinely uplifting.
Super Esham; Kindred spirit.

MAN OF STEEL

Remember me I leave a legacy,
A true superhero; not a false ideology.
Strengthened by His grace; protected by mercy,
He flies with me as I complete my journey.
The man who inspires with his art,
The man who touched a million hearts.
Very strong minded; very strong willed,
Esham Abdul, the man of steel.

esham abdul giles

Chapter Two: Tribulations

Please grant me peace, love and happiness for the rest of my LIFE!

EAG

esham abdul giles

The Rest of My LIFE

So much has gone on,
So much has been seen,
Countless friends Rest In Peace.

I'm in a zone.
Is it better to be left alone?
This heavy heart within,
All too soon, my brothers will never be forgotten.

How I feel, at times, miserable,
Thinking of distance, ready to take flight,
Free of despair for the rest of my life.

How would you feel?

Life is real,
We can't predict how things turn out.
I pray to GOD to grant me peace.
Only He can remove dark clouds.

Is there a place for me with decency?
No backbiting or betrayal,
Seek and you shall find,
Live In Peace for the rest of my life.

esham abdul giles

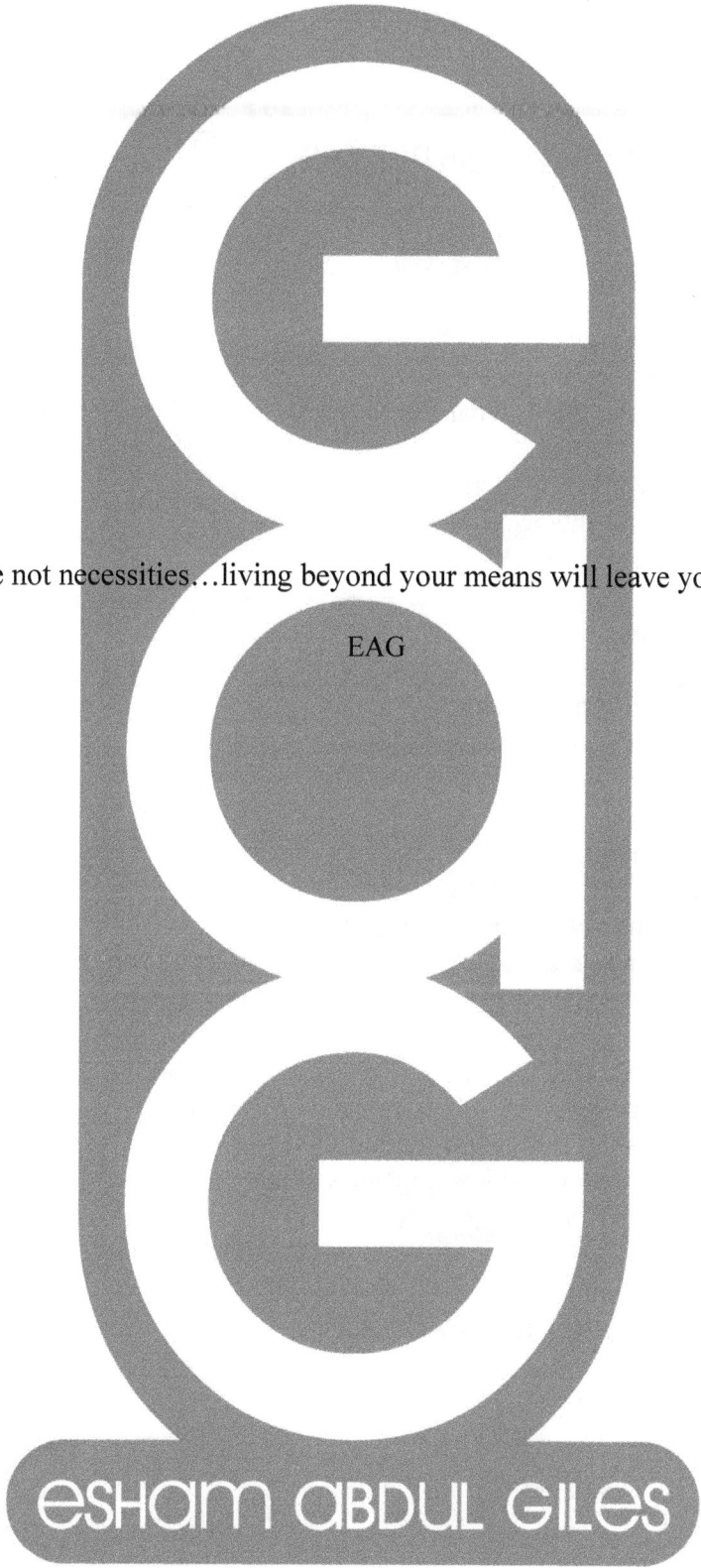

Luxuries are not necessities...living beyond your means will leave you empty.

EAG

BEER POCKETS CHAMPAGNE DREAMS

I want it all regardless of anything,
No matter the cost,
I live for the floss,
Clothes, jewelry, luxury cars,
Fine dining and drinks in upscale bars,
Pay check evaporated this is what I'm living for.

Priorities, bills I will get to later,
Need new clothes for the occasion.
This is where it's at.

Champagne dreams,
Beer pockets,
My ends don't justify my means,
Designer label, fine shoe game, cell phone,
BLING!

The baby needs a tutor,
I will worry about that in the future,
I need to see my money; make my baby cute,
Ugg boots or Prada sneaks,
My baby will be as stylish as me.

Gas and electric bill,
No life insurance policy,
No emergency stash or retirement account.
Struggling to buy groceries doesn't mean a thing.
Because I live for the floss,
No matter the cost,
Regardless of anything,
Beer pockets won't stop Champagne dreams.

esham abdul giles

I know I'll have more trying times in life, but the next time someone says, "DON'T FORGET EVERYTHING HAPPENS FOR A REASON", I'll know it's true. We all go through challenges in life. The important thing to know is that sooner or later the reason for your trials will come to you. When that happens you will find yourself better off than you did before.

EAG

esham abdul giles

REASONS

There is an underlying reason for everything. Walk with me as we gather some of my reason.

There's a reason that on September 4th, 1972 a child was born premature. As he grows, he endures so much good and bad. There's a reason that at 17 years of age, the boy becomes the father and has to grow up over night. There is a reason that on the eve of Thanksgiving 1991 one of his closest friends was taken so soon. There's a reason why time moves on and so many questions are left in doubt or unanswered. There's a reason why a Mother is left to bare a burden of being the only one left with her Mother and Brother have both been called to the heavens. There's a reason why in January of 2000 the bright lights have completely blown out as the running and the hustle have completely drained his legs.

There's a reason why in June 2002 the man walked across a stage with a great sense of accomplishment as he receives his Degree. There's a reason why a man has made so many foolish and unwise choices as he learns the fate of things the hard way. There's a reason why a man was once married and had terrible ending but a beautiful start. There's a reason why the man mourns yet again two more childhood friends that have been taken too soon. There's a reason why so much uncertainty is in this man as he is in a constant state of flux. There's a reason why GOD wants this man here, yet to be fully determined as the man finds his way. There's a reason why the man wrote this poem and there is a reason why you're reading it. GOD Bless!

esham abdul giles

32

Not knowing when to let go means that you've already lost.

EAG

The Struggle to Deal with the Hustle

As my brothers struggle to deal with the hustle,
The Life becomes nothing but a constant tussle,
At the highest point we think we have what it takes,
All to end up surround by a bunch of snitches, ruthless villains and many fakes.
All the fancy items make us seen;
We never stop to think that the DEA could be watching everything.
We don't sit in an untouchable position; pay attention,
We can't make this a legal business.

As my brothers struggle to deal with the hustle,
The Life becomes nothing but a constant tussle,
I stand high on center stage,
I live for today,
Carefree to anything that comes my way.
Authorities come to grant me a short stay,
Turned out to be several decades.

I'm back on the street; a convicted felon,
No meaningful employment.
Thinking drug dealing is my only weapon,
Create wealth fast without question.
No one can place an hourly wage on me,
I'm here to regain my title,
King of these streets.

As my brothers struggle to deal with the hustle,
The Life becomes nothing but a constant tussle,
I stack my money; I'm back on my grind,
I'm making smart moves they can't possibly catch me this time,
I'm going to keep on grinding; keep on pushing,
If they do run down on me I'm sitting on several millions.

esham abdul giles

As my brothers struggle to deal with the hustle,
The Life becomes nothing but a constant tussle,
Thinking to myself, "the money, women and
cars all were nice", but wait! "I don't need
to think too much because I'm sitting in this
cell for the rest of my life."

As I am this brother who can't knock the hustle.
I should've let go but was caught in the struggle.

esham abdul giles

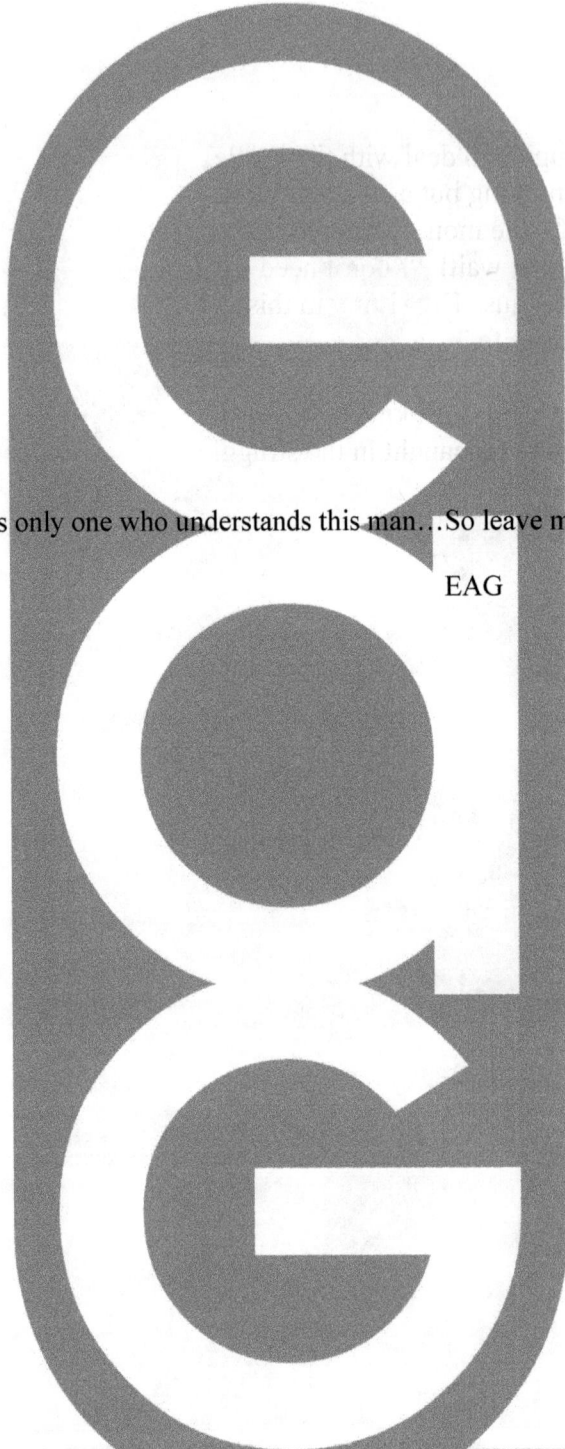

There is only one who understands this man…So leave me alone.

EAG

esham abdul giles

THE TWO SIDES OF ME

We make the world in which we live
by what we gather and what we give,
By our daily deeds and the things we say,
By what we keep or cast away.
We make our world by the beauty we see
or the HULK self imposed torture wrangling secrets inside of me.

This is why we meditate;
The ocean grants us lengthy escape,
Natural state; Natural space.
Leaving worldly things behind; the moon on rise,
 Stars brighten the midnight sky.
Tranquility; our peace of mind.

The life we lead, is all about peace,
But there are folks who try to release,
The angry side that dwells in me,
The rage and uncertainty,
Brutish force, so leave me be.

We make our world by the goals we pursue,
By the heights we seek and visualizing the higher view,
By hopes and dreams that reach the sun
And a will to fight until PEACE is won.

Disturbances take me to a place long familiar,
The deadly zone, the silent killer.
Release him free,
He'll bring the peace,
Colossal giant ready for reckoning,
Smashing all that threatens me.

esham abdul giles

37

What is the place in which we dwell;
 it's our fate, our heaven and hell.
All people see is when we smile and gleam
Not knowing of all the rage and anger that lives inside of me.
We gather and scatter, we take and we give,
We make our world – and there we live.
The two sides of me
I keep calm so HULK isn't let free.

esham abdul giles

In no way can I simply live a life without concern and care. I have to be able to contribute to my family, my neighborhood, my community. I have to leave a mark. I have to leave a legacy.
I HAVE TO BE DIFFERENT.

EAG

DIFFERENCES

There is a different kind of man, who resides here,
Never ashamed of who I am,
Knowledge of self and all surroundings,
Praise be to GOD for understandings.

General Patton, General Lee,
There's so much more to U.S. History,
Buffalo Soldiers; 25th Infantry,
Some may see this differently.
All History runs deep,
12th Century AD,
The war is HOLY,
The Crusaders, Knights Templar vs. Saladin.

If you haven't realized I am different yet,
Let me give you some more things to witness,
Different worlds; Different beliefs,
That makes neither one of us better than the other,
It makes us unique.

I wasn't brought into this world not to pay attention,
A leader born on a natural mission,
There's more to my world than just the community I live in,
I can't live a life of foolishness or transgression.

Diverse, divergent, contrary,
We live many different ways,
I'm here to say,
"Just because you're different you're not a castaway."

esham abdul giles

The subconscious mind is a part of you that knows more about yourself than you do. Why is this? We walk through this world in a lowered state of consciousness. There are deep memories, experiences, and understandings within our mind that have yet to be and may never be revealed.

I sit and reflect on unresolved matters in my life: deep hopes, worries, unrealized aspirations. Can there possibly be a place deep in my mind where I can see? Please grant me a moment of clarity.

EAG

esham abdul giles

DEEP IN MY MIND

I have relived so many things in my mind that I have no idea any more what's real & what are nightmares. I spend so much of my time thinking about things that happened in my life time as far back as 20 years ago & yet I worry that in that time they've been made out to be worse than they were. I don't know how to let things go & my mind keeps playing them all back at me over & over again & again. I truly believe that my mind is trying to drive me crazy..... I think that maybe I should just give up sometimes, crawl into my comfort zone, cut off the world and go at all things alone. Do I want to let things go? Should I let things go? This is what has made me...This is who I am. Some call me cold, I call myself strong. Some say I'm nonchalant or aloof. Why because I'm quiet and reserved? If you know me I'm always in deep thought.

esham abdul giles

And ALLAH found you lost and guided you.

Qur'an, Surah ad Dhuha 93:7

esham abdul giles

THE FLOOD

The Flooding has begun,
Despair, broken hearts, helplessness is everywhere.
Death of a loved one; the pain of divorce or severed relationship; losing a job.
We are in the flood.

The water has over run.
Some of us are facing a serious illness or disease,
This is realness not TV; some of us can't move or wiggle our feet,
The water runs too deep.
We are planted in the flood.

Living alone; living with regret,
Some of us never get over it,
The water's rising up, throw in the life jacket.
The water is taking me under.
I see hands but no one will reach out and grab mine,
I'm running out of time.
I'm drowning in this flood.

Constant thoughts run deep;
The water is swallowing me…what can I do?

I'm in the flood.

Can this Government get things in order at least once?
Homes are being lost; do to insurmountable cost,
I lost my job and all insurance,
Now I'm swimming with the sharks.
My Lord found me lost; he pulled me up with one call,
"BELIEVE!"
I won't leave you lost at sea,
I place no more than you can handle,
Let your faith guide you, as this is my answer.
The water shall recede,
Thank you Lord for believing in me; my feet are set free,
Drowning is not an option because I BELIEVE!

esham abdul giles

44

There is a tide in the affairs of men, Which taken at the flood, leads on to fortune. Omitted, all the voyage of their life is bound in shallows and in miseries. On such a full sea are we now afloat. And we must take the current when it serves, or lose our ventures.

William Shakespeare

esHam abduL GILes

I often wonder if she knows how I really feel at times.

EAG

esham abdul giles

The thought of being without her.

When I think of her I wonder how my life would be without her.

She has caused me so much pain; if I leave her I know I will miss her.

I can't help to think this way. She has made me feel so isolated at times.

As I reminisce I think of all the good times we shared,

I try to let that over shadow some of her jealous and hateful ways.

Even if I decide to leave her I will always love her.

So I say to her now, NEWARK!

You will always be part of me we share a love and a bond that can never be broken.

esham abdul giles

"Prophet Muhammad (SAWS) said, Whoever recites Surah al Waqiah at night would never encounter poverty."

Hadith

Shaitan threatens you with poverty and orders you to commit evil deeds; whereas Allah promises you Forgiveness from Himself and Bounty, and Allah is All Sufficient for His creatures' needs, All Knower.

Qur'an, Surah al Baqara 2:268

esham abdul giles

POVERTY STRICKEN

From the Great Depression to the war in Vietnam, The Reagan and Bush Administrations, poverty is deep seeded and from the looks of things it will never be gone. Rapidly increasing amounts of debt, high job losses, skyrocketing gas prices, food prices and a tidal wave of foreclosures, we are in the mist of financial ruin. We are poverty stricken.

Poverty is Politics, poverty is method and poverty is being a cut throat, as fat cats on Wall Street squabble and scheme, you have mother sitting in a dim kitchen and can't feed her child anything.

Poverty is oppression, depression, lack of faith; lack of hope,

Poverty is my neighbor in the back alley shooting his dope.

Poverty is no healthcare; poverty is welfare, the stealer of dreams,

Poverty makes me think I won't amount to anything.

Poverty is despair and despondence on hard working faces

Poverty is a father going to a dead end job as he hates this.

Poverty is man desperately seeking his mission,

While his wife and child wait in long lines to eat at soup kitchens.

Poverty is pressure; poverty is stress, everyday waking up to the same damn mess of hopelessness and helplessness.

As I pray and work hard to manifest my dreams,

I ask GOD to give fruit to us all and put an end to this poverty.

esham abdul giles

CREATE! INSTEAD OF LIVING OFF THE BACKS OF OTHERS THINKING
YOU'RE ABOVE US.

esHam aBDUL GILes

ACCOUNTABILITY

You people crack me up when given a little authority,

Let us speak in black and white on how you are…CLEARLY!

You are used, just as you use,

Nothing but Company Henchmen,

Let me go on in detail of you and your position,

Low level management is all you really are,

Given a chance to lead you forget who you were the day before.

Finger pointing, harassing and threatening is all you do,

Keep on going, your so called smarts will get the corporation sued.

You claim to operate ethically and by the book,

Why don't you stand up to the person next to you?

You know and see that they continuously do employees wrong,

But instead you go along to get along.

Keep protecting your first class idiots,

You will see just how soon you all will be gone.

Some are scared to speak up, so they kiss your hand, to join your buddy band.

esham abdul giles

I will never belittle myself. I'm not a crony…I'M A MAN! Who will take a stand.

So you conjure up a plan to suspend or to permanently dismiss, as soon as you can.

Let me share something with you company man,

come for me if you'd like, I really don't give a DAMN!

You really don't get it; I will never present myself as someone above everyone else,

For title, privilege and small percentage, overtime with no compensation

Not even owning the business.

Let me share with you my position HENCHMEN,

I'm AUTHOR and CEO of my business,

Recouping 100% of the profits.

Instead of licking the boots of who you answer to, smiling hard and puckering up,

Take a good look at your company's code of ethics and professional conduct.

Until you stop being unethical, immoral, impotent people and having no one challenge you when you're wrong.

You will continue to be just what you are,

Low level management.

esham abdul giles

"I am not bound to win
but I am bound to be true;
I am not bound to succeed
but am bound to live up
to what light I have. "

Abraham Lincoln

ACCOUNTABILITY.

eag

esham abdul giles

It is my understanding that a shark is not an aide or helper but a PREDATOR.

EAG

eSHAM ABDUL GILES

LOAN SHARKS

School, home, car, I took care of business.

Wait! Economy fails. We need to amend this,

"Have you read the fine print by our underwriters and lenders?"

Yes, too late, after I've signed those seventy pages of bait and switch!

Loan approved with conditions?

AMERICA! Wake up and pay attention!

Don't sign away your life on those lines…

Watch out!

PREDATORY LENDERS as gangsta as any Blood, Crip, or Marasalvatrucha.

Education isn't free,

Neither is the white picket American dream,

Convinced to purchase a home as if the mortgage is all that you need to afford.

Sallie, Fannie, and Freddie are waiting patiently

For you to persuade yourself that credit scores need not be perfect before you take the dive.

esham abdul giles

Sharks in the ocean, sharks behind desks posing meek and helpful with a grin and a smile,

Waiting for you to graduate from junior ballers- clothes and electronics- to the real time- condos

and Benzes,

Fast talk, dreams, and a pen filled with blood

For you to sign over your life on the contract lines...

Your better mind sees that the math doesn't add up

Shark whispers, "Don't worry, in a few years you'll be able to finance and avoid that bubble
payment."

They make their percentage before you leave the table, they could care less.

Remember people this is a business,
You are the only one who can protect yourself and your best interests.

So, for the time being, tune them out,

Educate yourself, make a solid budget, before you purchase that house.

Know all of the rules before you commit to anything,

Learn to discern the SHARKS and their trade of, Predatory Lending.

esham abdul giles

56

Loan Sharks

Borrowing is not much better than begging; just as lending with interest is not much better than stealing.

Anonymous

eag

esham abdul giles

You lie, thieve and steal. You go to jail. You are no different than anybody else.

EAG

esham abdul giles

Federal Deception Illegal Corruption

In God we trust,
Money & Markets,
His Majesty should not be associated with these cowards.
They build you up, sell you dreams,
Give you reasons why you should invest,
My people listen, "There is no honor amongst thieves."

Out of touch fat cats, corporate jets,
Look at the salaries of these meaningless Execs.
Wall Street generals bring about destruction,
They try to calm you down claiming insurance,
When FDIC really stands for,
Federal, Deceiving, Illegal, Corruption.

Tyco, Enron companies shattered,
These jerks steal more cash than the mad hatter.
Stock market out of control, as losses mount,
Banks going swimming faster than trout.
The stock market is seen as a big scam,
You lock up Martha Stewart why not Alan Greenspan?

Horrendous damage has been done, the perils of an unregulated market,
There should have never been a trial for that guy who MADE -OFF.
65 Billion Stolen for twenty years,
Escort this scum to the nearest cliff.
Crime and Wall Street go hand and hand,
Every other week there is a new sham,
Most of the fraud you will never hear about,
If you invest, do so wisely as they will clean you out.

esham abdul giles

59

For those who tell us the economy is growing,
"Please tell me where you get your numbers?"
Stimulus programs are not going to bring recovery,
It is like pushing on a string, we do not have liquidity,
We have insolvency, which is accompanied by overcapacity.

Stop associating God with money and the corrupt stock market.

esham abdul giles

Seest thou not that Allah makes the clouds move gently, then joins them together, then makes them into a heap?—then wilt thou see rain issue forth from their midst. And He sendsdown from the sky mountain masses (of clouds) wherein is hail: Hestrikes therewith whom He pleases and He turns it away from whom Hepleases, the vivid flash of His lightning well-nigh blinds the sight.

Qur'an, Surah an Noor 24:43

esham abdul giles

STORM RETURNS

Weather radar speed past the sidebar,

The Storm returns fast with miraculous roar!

COO, CEO, Hedgefund Managers of sham and scam business,

Heavy winds blow the roof and you out of those offices.

Don't try and pick up and run,

Like you do on everyone,

I'm going to burn your pockets faster than casinos in the sun.

STORM RETURNS

What can you do for me, honestly?

You live in a land of make believe,

I live in reality.

Move on and do whatever you choose,

You and I both know I'm not the one for you.

Your progression is slow, misty rain,

I move with force, category 5 hurricane.

esham abdul giles

STORM RETURNS

Hey weatherman in Washington D.C. Report the forecast,

There is a tornado sweeping thru Congress,

Moving rapidly to the left leaving a destruction of garbage.

STORM RETURNS

Heavy hitters, so –called drug dealers, hood celebrities, Social media A listers,

Since your brain is limited to the bubble that surrounds you,

We have no use,

Be gone hollow frames…TYPHOON!

STORM RETURNS

Slander, propaganda you act like it's fun,

You only speak good things of Forty One and his Son.

Check this here little man in news land and your band of fools,

"A FOX can't out slick lighten…Thunderous BOOM!"

esham abdul giles

STORM RETURNS

Speakers of the books, who betray, lie and deceive,

Don't worry about me,

There's a storm waiting underneath your feet.

STORM RETURNS

No need to wonder why I grouped all of together,

You are deserving of this bad weather.

No radar can detect what's coming next,

Cloudy, with a chance of pain if you commit to foolishness.

esham abdul giles

"You won't worry about healthcare for everyone until it's you or your family member who's sick…try trading positions with many Americans who can't afford healthcare."

Message to Congress from Esham Abdul Giles

If the United States is such a great super power, why can't we afford to fund Health Care for every American, a fundamental human right? What the HELL!!!

"Its' not just an expensive privilege for a few!"

esham abdul giles

HEALTHCARE

Health is not a care, it's a right,
Will these fools ever see the light?
People are dying 45,000 each year,
Simply from not having Health Care.
This is a shame and damned travesty,
Will your dream live on Senator Ted Kennedy?

As he was the most stalwart fighter for equal health care,
The lion of the senate, these other fools just don't get it.
Republican after Republican, spreading lie after lie,
Keep the public on death panels as there is no compromise.
Those Democrats driving this plan no doubt have good intentions,
but do they have courage?

Let's get Health Care for each and every American.
As the President deals with this circus each day,
I know he grows frustrated that the momentum is not going his way.
Healthcare premiums have soared because healthcare inflation is nearly triple the
overall inflation rate,
Make Politicians pay the bill if you have a hospital stay.

Take a look at Canada this can be done,
We can have Health Care in the U.S. for everyone.
Death in this value system is not the end of a journey, but a rotten break,
Take a look at the numbers State by State.

This is the land of opportunity, where everyone has the God-given right to thrive
and prosper.

It's also the land of the second chance, a place for the self-made and remade man,
so why in the hell doesn't everyone have Health Insurance?
Like Senator Ted Kennedy we must keep up the fight,
Health is not a care, it's our right.

esham abdul giles

66

For me, this is a season of hope, new hope for a justice and fair prosperity for the many and not just for the few, new hope. And this is the cause of my life, new hope that we will break the old gridlock and guarantee that every American -- north, south, east, west, young, old -- will have decent, quality health care as a fundamental right and not a privilege.

Senator Ted Kennedy Speech at 2008 Democratic National Convention Aug 26, 2008

esham abdul giles

So much to gain, everything to lose… I don't know who came up with the fairytale that says, "You can't miss anything that you never had."
 That's a lie! I'm missing my millions.

EAG

esham abdul giles

THE MANHATTAN PROJECT

Trust and believe, time has a way of returning,

And if you don't plan accordingly it's your future you are ruining.

Foolish investments in meaningless crap,

Cars, clothes, jewelry did it all in my twenties…believe that!

And still came up with a plan to protect,

I will state my claim on the free market,

I call it, THE MANHATTAN PROJECT.

Internet boom! 1994, I need to be a part of,

Time to blow up big! NUCLEAR!

Commodities stocks, bonds, dotcom's,

 Oppenheimer funds,

Wall Street Journal tucked under my arm.

My outlook is big investments,

Paying close attention to that small block in lower Manhattan.

52 week high, 52 week low,

I'm not worried a bit though.

esham abdul giles

The Commander and Chief,

Has the national spending budget at a surplus.

Great news for the economy,

I will be rich by 30.

But that time has come, now the Bush Administration is in office,

Profits turn to losses.

Thousands gone in this market.

Angry, ready to protest,

This President and his baffled House of Congress,

I will get this money back with interest.

I'm rattled but I' m determined to multiply what remains.

The market schooled me.

Over aggressive investing builds your ego. It's sexy, cool, and smart when it pays.

At the other side of the game stands a experienced and more mature investor.

Profits pulled and protected.

Don't be fooled, I may have been down,

But, I've never been out.

esham abdul giles

Don't take your right to vote for granted…go out and make vote count at each and every election from school board to Presidential. If you don't, as your taxes and fees increase and services diminish and you or your neighbor gets laid off, you really will regret your apathy.

EAG

THE GOVERNOR'S MANSION

Answer these questions while you sit up in the people's mansion?

You know what? I don't even know why I'm asking,

You can't even stay awake during a rock and roll concert

To respond to my queries not only requires that you have a conscience but are alert.

Your fifteen minutes are up!

Everyone I know is tired of you cutting positions.

Run for your health instead of bullying politicians.

Trust this; you and I both know you got into office on classic manipulation, duplication.

He said, "Change" and won,

You said "Change" and won.

Folks thought that you both would work to improve their lives.

You duped them son.

Police, teachers, and firefighters casting ballots against their own interests.

I know damn well that I didn't vote for you!

I guess you said, "I'll define unnecessary spending as health benefits, pension, disability, and traditional public schools."

The folks who marched me into office, my first targets.

esham abdul giles

Their pride will assuage their rage. Blame it all on falling economic markets.

Slow to protest being shafted, that'd require them to acknowledge that they had been fooled.

I care about the people that you cut off and screwed.

Your time is limited; the Zombie electorate is wounded but awake,

Soon someone else will be Governor of the state.

esham abdul giles

In my 15 minutes of fame I have a lot to say!

EAG

esham abdul giles

BE HEARD

I write to express,
I speak to be heard,
I'm talking loud in a crowd,
Why won't anyone listen?
Give me straight answers,
Elected Politician.
People need help,
You sit at your table to discuss jobless numbers,
We are out here dying from hunger.
You knock on doors to manipulate our vote,
When you get in office there's nothing to show.
People need jobs we have mouths to feed,
We will have them if you stop all the greed.
You claim there is nothing we can do, we have budget cuts,
So tell me why did another Politician leave out in handcuffs?
I'll tell you why because he was arrogant and corrupt.
The people who need help rarely see your face,
What a damn disgrace.
Don't shake my hand or promise me anything,
I have a Degree and can make my own means.
But there are people, who suffer and need you to listen,
Give us straight answers Mr. Politician.
As you scramble and carefully craft your words,
People already know that you're throwing a curve.
I got something for you Mr. Politician, a verse from Proverbs,
"The word that is heard perishes, but the letter that is written remains."
As this was written to be heard.

esham abdul giles

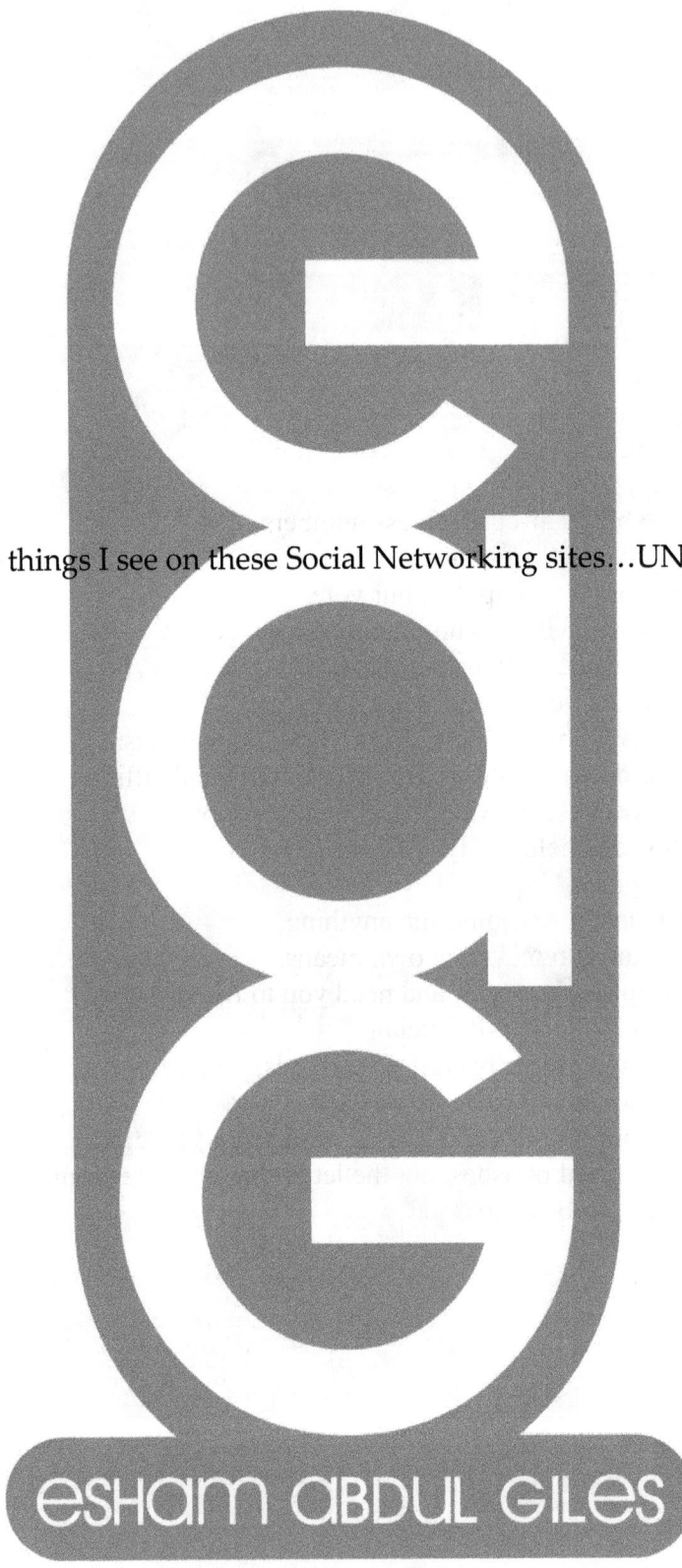

The things I see on these Social Networking sites…UNREAL!

EAG

SOCIAL SECURITY

The need to be stuck in this thing

We call Social Networking,

Never seems to amaze me.

Most people don't use it meaningfully,

Go on sites to look for love or to pretend to be something other than their true identity.

The need to be stuck in this thing,

Social Security.

You can't stand to look this woman in the face at the Masjid, why are you sending her a friend request?

If you are a pacifist in the street, who is the five star general on your page?

Tell the truth, share your raw opinion, keep it funky, keep it 100 when you write on these walls.

That's my challenge. Who hears my call?

Your heart will be broken if your cyber friends and family find out who you really are?

Remember, "Life is not lived behind your computer screen."

Use your forum to share information and truths and gainful things.

Leave the security of make believe.

esham abdul giles

77

I don't claim to be nothing but me,

In this age of synthetic connections.

Creating a forum for truth and knowledge,

Giving honest insight on things I been through and things that bother.

Not checking in my present location,

Or who's doing what or dating who,

That's not what you'll get here so don't waste your follow.

I use social media responsibly,

Not a means to be celebrity or have some sort of popularity.

I think before I post. Because everything isn't for everybody

Add that statement to your Security of Social Networking.

eSHɑM ɑBDUL GILES

Trust me, "those who lie aren't lying to anyone but themselves."

EAG

esham abdul giles

LIAR BEWARE

We are many and you are few, we listen to the crap you spew. Don't think we aren't up to speed, on truth and lies as you deceive. You spout out lines of twisted tales, like politicians or shady stock deals. You exchange the truth for what we would like to hear, while your treachery knows no fear. You are what's wrong in every way, no longer care about what you say. You paint your picture so distorted, you create the facts so that the honest story not reported. You bend the facts for your own gain, how is it that you feel no pain? Just when you think all is well and you have won, Allah only knows how you will answer to all deception. Shaytan is waiting! He will embrace you with open arms. Go ahead and lie, in fact, sing your song LIAR!!!

esham abdul giles

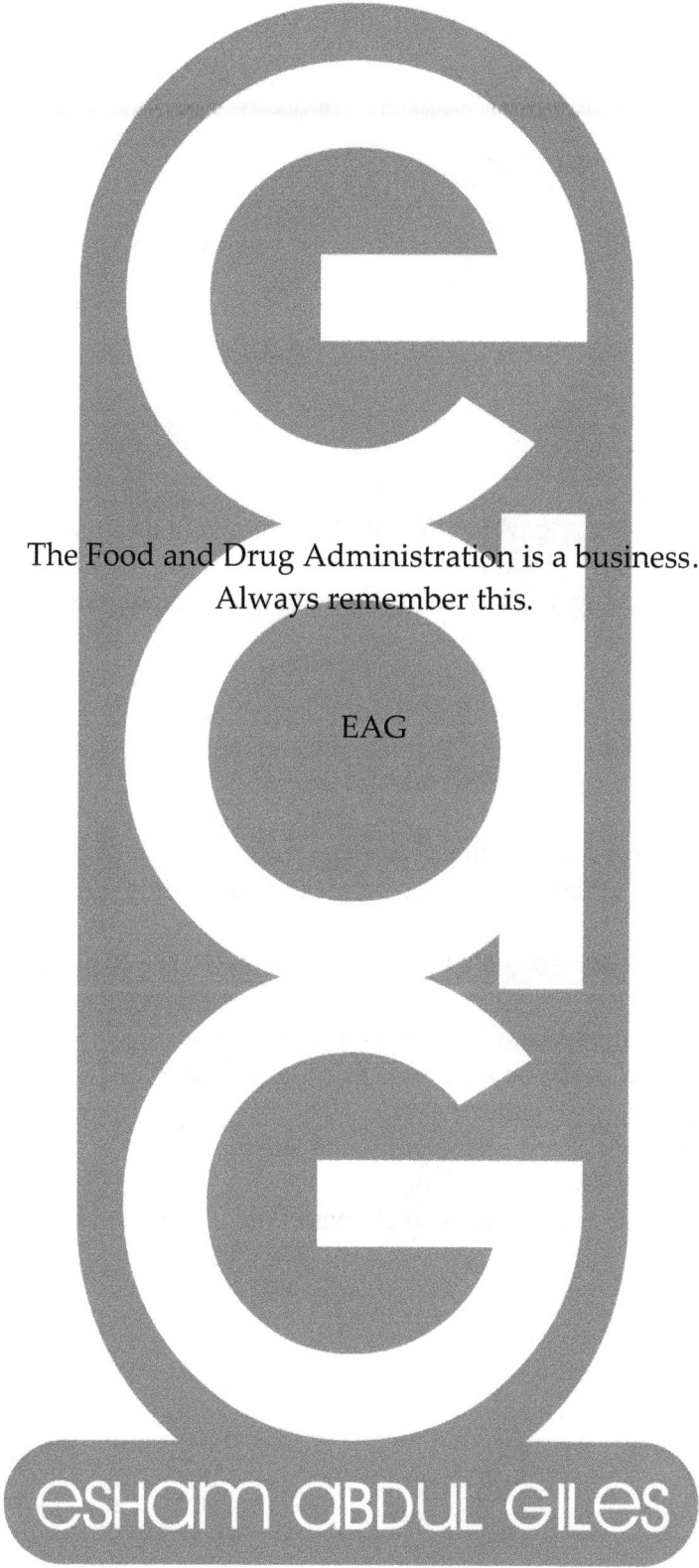

The Food and Drug Administration is a business…
Always remember this.

EAG

<u>FDA</u>

Food and Drug Administration

We Eat
We Drink
We Take
Based solely on what they say
Yay or Nay,
Some of us any way.
If it's not approved
I won't choose,
I don't know what's going ON with half of the food and drugs we consume any
way
So why run even a bigger risk of using something not approved by the FDA?

I'll tell you why
We want to be high,
We want to look nice,
We want to eat foreign things and don't think twice

So Food and Drug Administration, I ask you this,
"Are these bioengineered foods and new medications doing more harm than
good?"
 You recall and quote, "The data was misrepresented. The long term effects were
misunderstood."
Understatement is the word, big time! Don't you think?
FDA decision makers as you sit there and contemplate
Stage three approvals we patiently wait.
I, Myself and Double R are vested with high stakes,
Dub it, Operation WIN!
Because after all, your make up is solely based on give and take.

My friends of FDA.

eSHAM ABDUL GILES

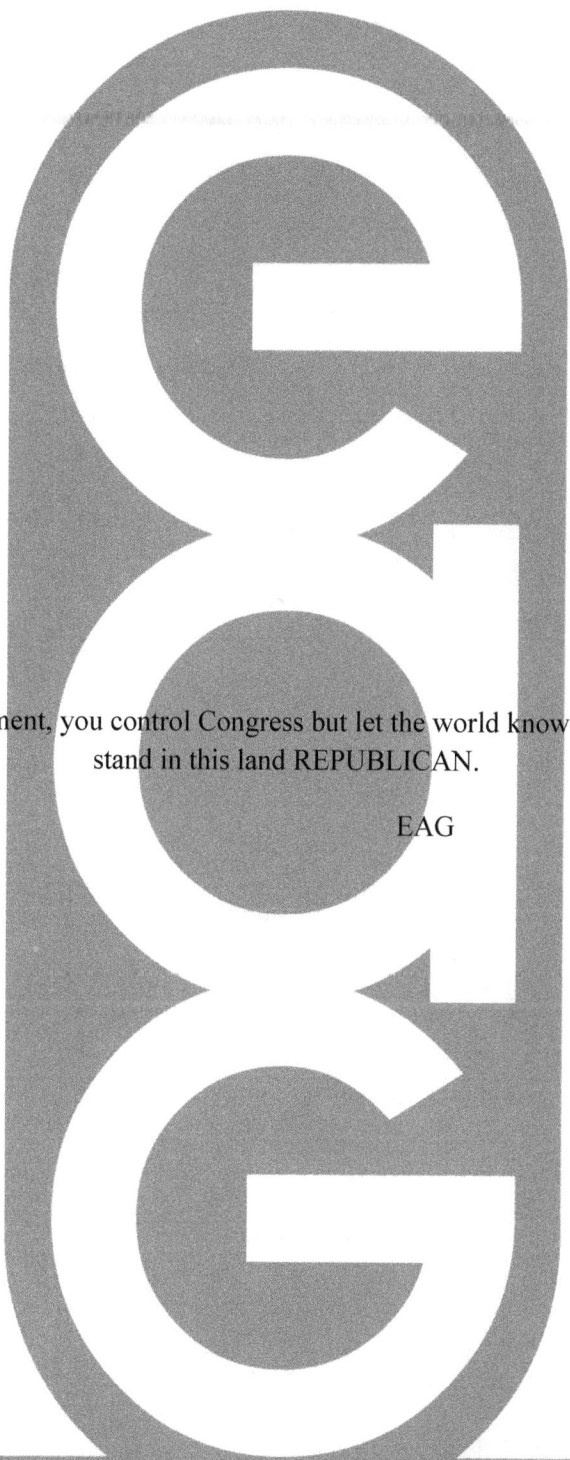

Divided Government, you control Congress but let the world know where you really
stand in this land REPUBLICAN.

EAG

esham abdul giles

Where do you stand Republican?

State by state; all you Washington folk

You try to rewrite history and the United States Constitution,

I have problems with you on many levels,

But go ahead and slam your gavel.

Let us hear it, go on and draw your distinction,

Denied!!!

Equality vs. Inequality.

Go on RNC lie, lie, lie!

Saving defense budgets and cutting programs for the defenseless is your position.

You idiotic panel, I couldn't make up this shameless counterproductive stage play.

Saving the rich is where you stand Republican

War on the middle class and poor is all you have in store.

I challenge you to common sense

Most of you lack conviction and dedication;

"There are no permanent friends or enemies in politics, just permanent interests,"

Don't know how you convinced the people to vote you in.

You lack authenticity.

esham abdul giles

Do you know how important it is that math and science make the world work?

I think not; Education budgets trashed and teachers fired while you chase down sports figures for things, like steroids, you claim to know all about.

The average man could solve many issues on half your salary REPUBLICAN'T!

"Our primary goal is to make sure that he is a one term President."

The level of attempts and incoherence

Some of us see you for who you truly are; responsibilities is not your policy

Taxpayer money to save your jobs,

scandal after scandal, you are the biggest frauds.

The fact is you bring about backwards thinking and ultimate destruction

Don't know what planet you conservatives live on; you only protect your interest,

Fraudulent conservatives.

The elephant in the room truly fits your crew, RNC,

You cannot win this

The record of your time; is lies, lies, lies.

esham abdul giles

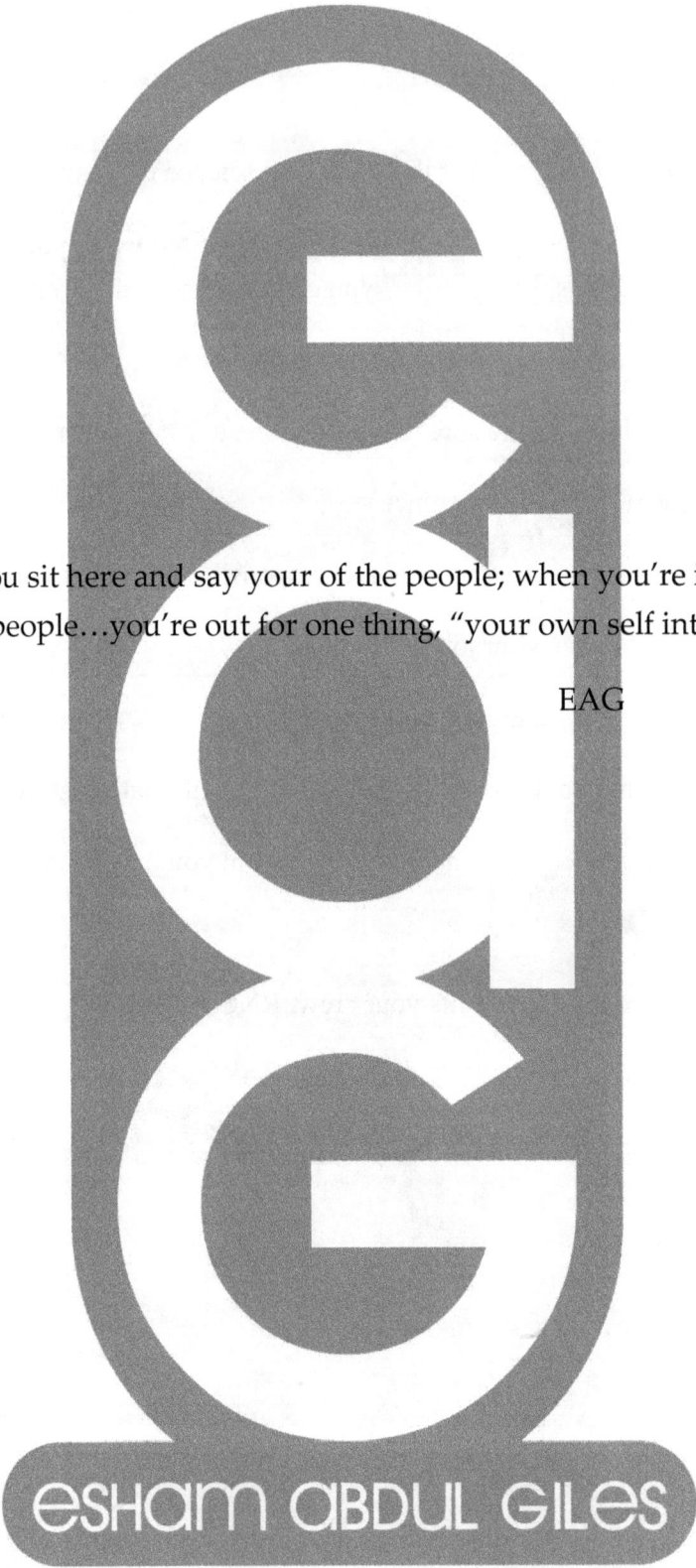

How can you sit here and say your of the people; when you're in reality not for the people…you're out for one thing, "your own self interest."

EAG

eSHAM ABDUL GILES

PROFITS AND PRINCIPLES

Focus Write Inspire!

I am building on a system of understanding and self determination,

Totally a force for good,

Presenting myself in a positive light as only one should,

Giving back to my community as much as I could.

I know my history and the price we paid,

To have freedom and ownership,

Not self centered, but self made.

Thieves, scammers and get over's control and rape.

TAKE! TAKE! TAKE!

Not giving those you employee a meaningful wage.

This is not why our leaders paved the way,

You crooks have no shame.

Forget and or crush where you come from…Total DISGRACE!

You offer and suggest how I should suck the well dry,

Your job is to belittle and keep down,

Mine is progress and INSPIRE.

esham abdul giles

MIND your own business

Don't tell me how to do mine,

You do your thing exploiting women and glorifying crimes.

As your popularity grows and principles go,

The meaningless profits you make aren't moral,

You give nothing back to the community you stole.

Take this here is a practical lesson,

A code of conduct,

As you build your brand in that very neighborhood you come from.

Life is about teaching and preparing our young…letting them see and be proud of where they come from.

Elders looking on us with a sense of happiness filled with pride.

Giving back to the community and not robbing it blind.

esham abdul giles

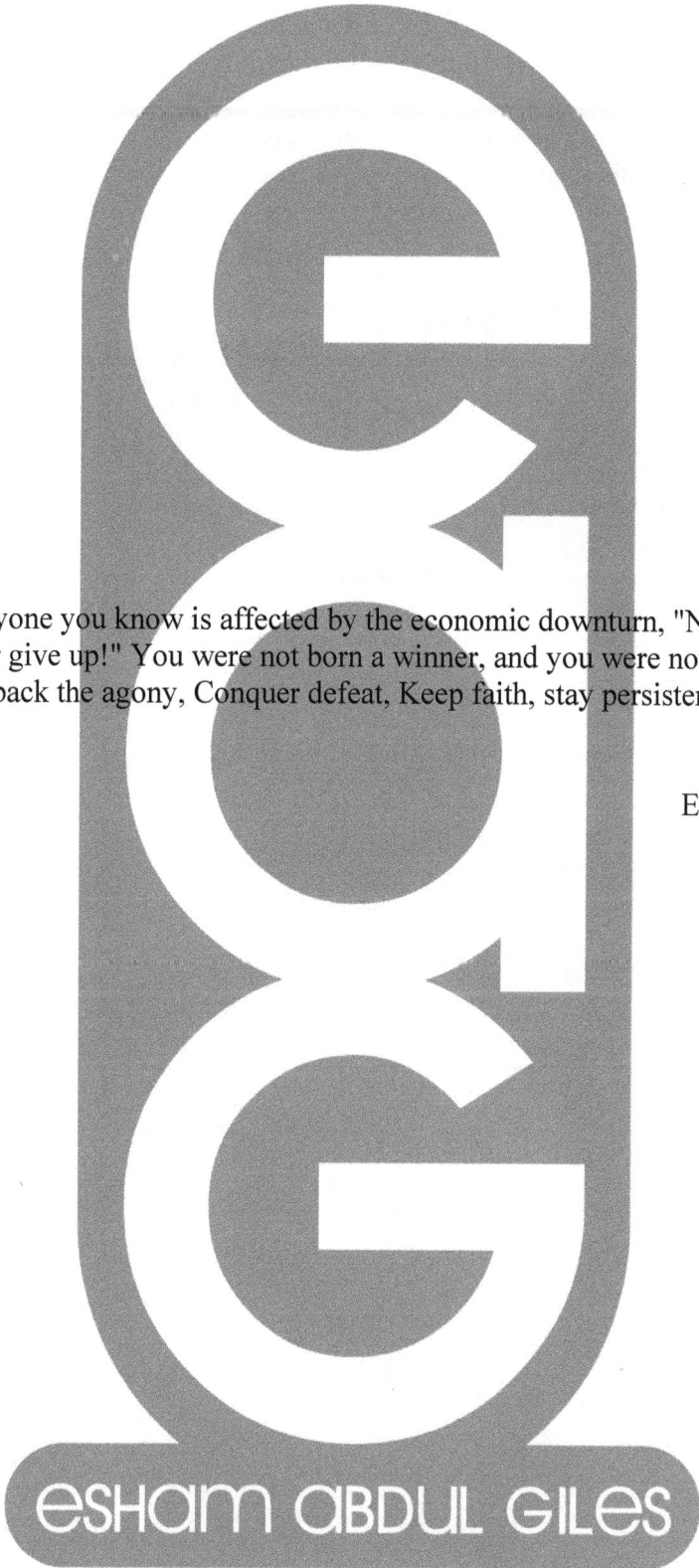

If you or anyone you know is affected by the economic downturn, "Never Quit, never, never give up!" You were not born a winner, and you were not born a loser. Push back the agony, Conquer defeat, Keep faith, stay persistent and you will win.

EAG

esham abdul giles

AGONY OF DEFEAT

I'm feeling the agony of defeat I need protection,
Especially during this recession,
There are no exceptions,
For any of my actions,
I stand alone,
Praying to Allah let this feeling go away.

I'm feeling the agony of defeat,
No need to mention,
What an exception,
Of fighting depression,
Working on my corrections,
Yet still pointing myself in the wrong directions.

I'm feeling the agony of defeat,
I need peace,
A way to release,
I need to retreat,
I can't even sleep,
These weak faith feelings that repeat,
Head down and heart closed
I cannot defeat the agony.

esham abdul giles

I want to escape this place…just for a minute, or some time, even if it's just a thought in my mind.

EAG

esham abdul giles

ESCAPE FROM PERDITION

Darkness covers this place
High murder rates
I have to find a way to escape; can't go on at this pace
Ambulance continuously running thru the night and day
I dread this forsaken place…
No direction, I wander alone
Leaving behind this so-called home…
Each moment quickly overlaps
Time fast forwards through my past and fading grasp…
As my reality is unmasked.
Anger grips my heavy soul
No one knows the Hurt…of the greatest pain I've known…
Happiness and hope long since gone
With my head hung low I stumble on…
Constant loss, rage in my heart, screams in my ears
Filling my eyes with many years of tears…
The two sides of me want to conclude
In that dark room of solitude
I place my face within heavy hands
I wonder who or if anyone understands…
That I'm a tired man.
I close my eyes to finally ask
For freedom from this inescapable mess…
I awake, Oh Allah, please grant me escape
As yet another day in Perdition has begun!

esham abdul giles

7: Be not deceived; God is not mocked: for whatsoever a man soweth, that shall he also reap.

8: For he that soweth to his flesh shall of the flesh reap corruption; but he that soweth to the Spirit shall of the Spirit reap life everlasting.

9: And let us not be weary in well doing: for in due season we shall reap, if we faint not.

GALATIANS 6: 7-9 (KJV) KING JAMES VERSION

esham abdul Giles

HEARTBREAK

I've been cheated many times but I forgave,
At least on the surface anyway.
Because those whom came after would ultimately pay,
For something someone else did, I'm sorry to say.
I wasn't built like this from the start,
Anger, betrayal, lack of trust control my heart.
Material, beauty, curvaceous; what some call "a sight to see",
Stone HEART! I don't care,
It's very hard to convince me.

Not looking for revenge,
Or looking to break hearts,
But this is reality,
I know where I stand with many from the start.
Is this me; am I really living this life?
The ones I meet make me realize,
Satisfying self at the cost of what or whomever,
Is the ultimate prize!
We all are prone to HEARTBREAK!

Twelve years she gave,
I know why she stayed.
Believing in me and the thought of change,
Disappointment and lies is what I gave.
Broken hearted because in my gut I really cared,
Please believe what I say,
My reasons maybe my excuses for my betrayal.
I did many wrongs in past days,
Victim became the victimizer,
ALLAH please remove this disdain and recklessness from me.
Please apply the brakes,
No more collisions that lead to HEARTBREAK.

esham abdul giles

94

So **As** I say please forgive me,
By your side on many trying days I would be.
I never meant for things to end up this way,
There is a special place and part of you that will stay.
Peace, love, and prayers from the owner of HEARTBREAK.

esham abdul giles

Divorce can trigger a wide range of actions and emotions…trust issues, anger, rejection, betrayal, fear, loneliness and social isolation. All of these emotions can cause stress and distract people from concentrating fully on another relationship especially the prospect of a new marriage…Some say that people who don't move past being hurt are afraid of commitment. I beg to differ. Having felt the pain and disappointment of a broken nuptial bond, I wouldn't look at other folks who have experienced the same trial expecting them to make a commitment again…let alone marriage.

EAG

esham abdul giles

Can I possibly love again?

As I sit in this court ready to go home,
Thinking to myself I'm about to be all alone.
I would never want to keep anyone by force,
But, why in the world would she want to divorce?
My heart is broken; I'm holding so much anger,
Tell me why she did me like this,
Guess it's human nature.

I know there are many things for which I hold fault.
She finally got fed up,
Bringing our world to a screeching halt.
The Karma from my drama may have forced her to walk.
I sit at this table grasping my thoughts.

No need to love again.

Gravity is pushing. I'm pulling,
Esham, be patient,
I never want to be in this situation,
I will never love again.

As time passes and I try to date,
Soul holding on to anger and hate,
Thinking to myself, "this is a waste",
I definitely would undermine a relationship,
Can't she tell I'm so not interested?
I can't possibly love again.

But, wait, I see a vision, a stunning light,
I've been swimming in this flood so long
I can't possibly know how to deal.

esham abdul giles

97

But, wait, there is this warm and hopeful feeling for which I hold so much hate,
Esham, take the chance, step out on faith.
She's beautiful, supportive, and so many kind words,
Maybe I can love again but I don't want to be hurt.

Gravity is pushing and pulling and this time it must change,
She's not the one who caused you so much pain.
Ironically, I think she's digging me just the same,
I need to be sure, look in her face,
Is this really taking place?
Is she a mirage or an illusion?
Please bring my thoughts to a conclusion.
Tears drop from my eye down to my chin
She puts her gentle hands up to wipe them,
"I'm here for you, let go, and love again."

Love is meant to be embraced and shared. Not feared.
Don't fall victim to the state of loneliness, as this will cause you to make foolish,
desperate choices that you will surely regret.
Pray for what you want, be specific, be patient.
In time you will be granted what you desire.
You will experience LOVE for the first time or you will LOVE again.

esham abdul giles

98

Those who show patience, firmness and self-control; who are true (in word and deed); who worship devoutly; who spend (in the way of Allah); and who pray for forgiveness in the early hours of the morning.

Qur'an, Surah Aal-e- Imran 200:17

esham abdul giles

DARK ROOM OF SOLITUDE

I sit in the solitude of a dark room,
listening intently
for the sound of quiet
I wait patiently
for something that's not here
It's just another hollow frame
It's just another empty space
another empty moment
I will wait another year.
There's nothing to do
but listen to my thoughts
And they are empty as I feel
Often betrayed and hard fought.
I'm not a man who loves Drama, Issues, and Doubt
I am lonely and only one can help
for I am lost with myself
in my quiet space trying to figure things out
Here is where I pray for happiness to release its way out of
My dark room of solitude.

esham abdul giles

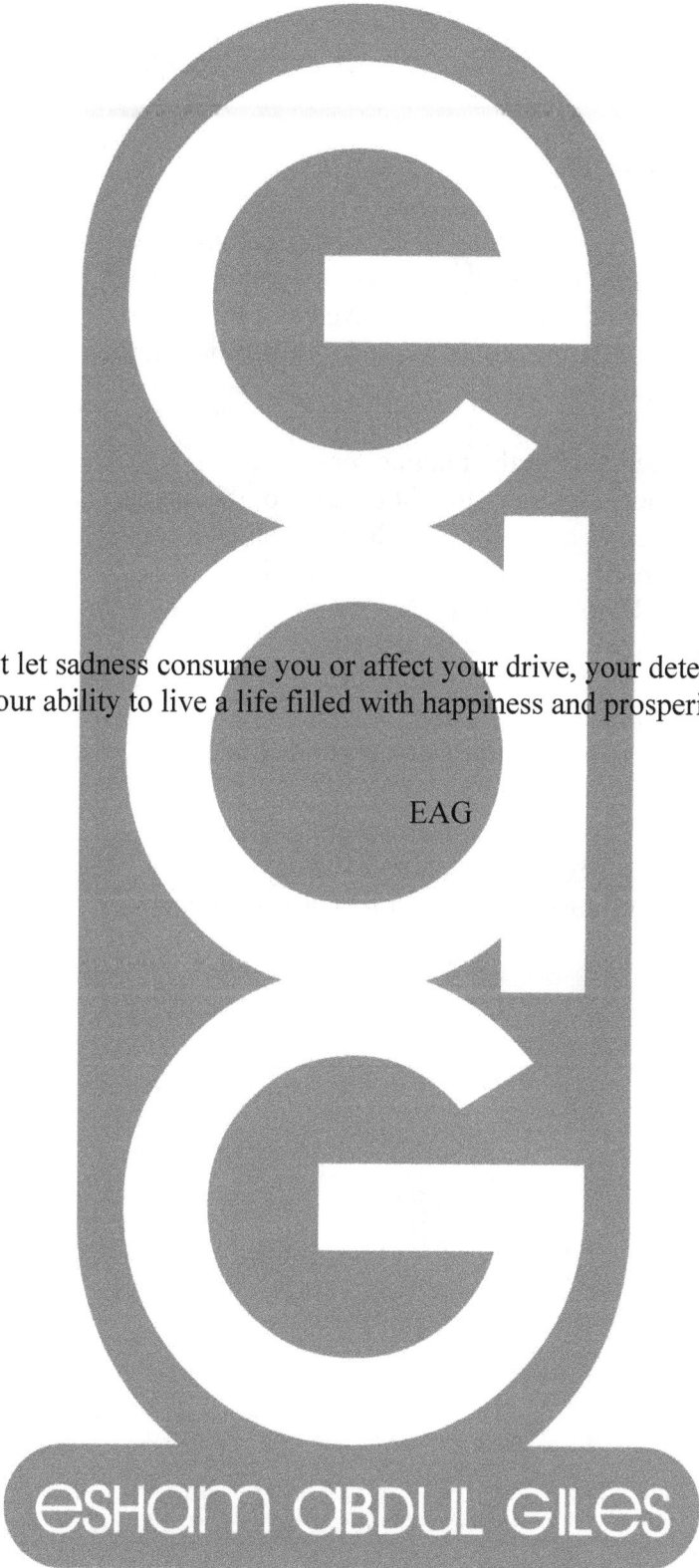

Please don't let sadness consume you or affect your drive, your determination or your ability to live a life filled with happiness and prosperity.

EAG

THE DREAMS OF A SAD MAN

Why is he sad?
Why can't his hurt past?
Can he possibly live beyond his dreams?
What he asks for is quiet and simple yet so difficult to receive.
He's constantly ripped and picked like a crow grabbing at his food.
He often feels taken advantage of and played as a fool.
All he wants is to be happy without agendas or preconditions,
Can the light he sees truly glisten?

Tired of all the drama no truth or admission,
Is it possible to meet someone straight up and not the representative?
Truth, Dare, and Consequence, this is the position he's constantly in.
TRUTH is a matter of just saying so why tell a lie?
Why does he DARE to take the risk?
When he already knew the CONSEQUENCE.

He Dreams, He Dreams, He Dreams
That sadness turns to happiness,
But his vision is truly never seen,
As it always tends to get dark with a nightmarish scene.
Until the day comes when it's a reality and not a dream,
He will and can only wait patiently for this despair to leave.

esham abdul giles

Chapter Five: Desires, Discernment, Discipline

There is someone out there for everyone…Regardless of what your likeness is. Being compatible ultimately wins.

EAG

esham abdul giles

COMPATIBILITY

Virgo on Virgo we are an evenly matched combination,
As I am over critical and so is she, yet
We would quietly, passively battle everyday of the week.

Virgo and Cancer this relationship can work,
They go hand and hand like water soils earth.

Virgo and Libra we couldn't be more different,
As I am reserved, she's out going; this could be a great position.
I try to stay serious at all times,
Libra's tendencies can help me unwind.

Virgo and Sagittarius the question with this is "for how long?"
And how long is too long, with these signs something will drastically go wrong.

Virgo and Aquarius the chemistry will not be too great and attraction more on the
Intellectual than the emotional and in time Aquarius will become frustrated and
bored.

Virgo and Leo, the Lion is a people's person, who seeks attention and appreciation
from all who
Are around them, I'm a much more quiet person, who believes in humility and
modesty.
I like consistency and she likes adventure and excitement,
don't get me twisted, nothing is wrong with this,
Just know now that she wouldn't be the first on my list.

Virgo and Capricorn we seem to be a harmonious pair,
The relationship will be loyal as this is what I want,
Can it possibly be with a Capricorn?

esham abdul giles

Virgo and Scorpio this combination works quiet well,
Never really experienced one so only time will tell.

Virgo and Pisces this match can go either way,
If Pisces is too sensitive I won't stay.

Virgo and Gemini together we will be thrilling,
As long as I can keep up with Gemini's constant mood swings.

Virgo and Taurus this is cool but not a pair made in heaven,
As Taurus thinks I'm too critical and always trying to teach her a lesson.

Virgo and Aries don't know if we can coexist,
As Aries thinks I'm too laid back and I think she's too aggressive.

I wrote this all in fun, but what if there is really some truth to this one

esHam abduL GiLes

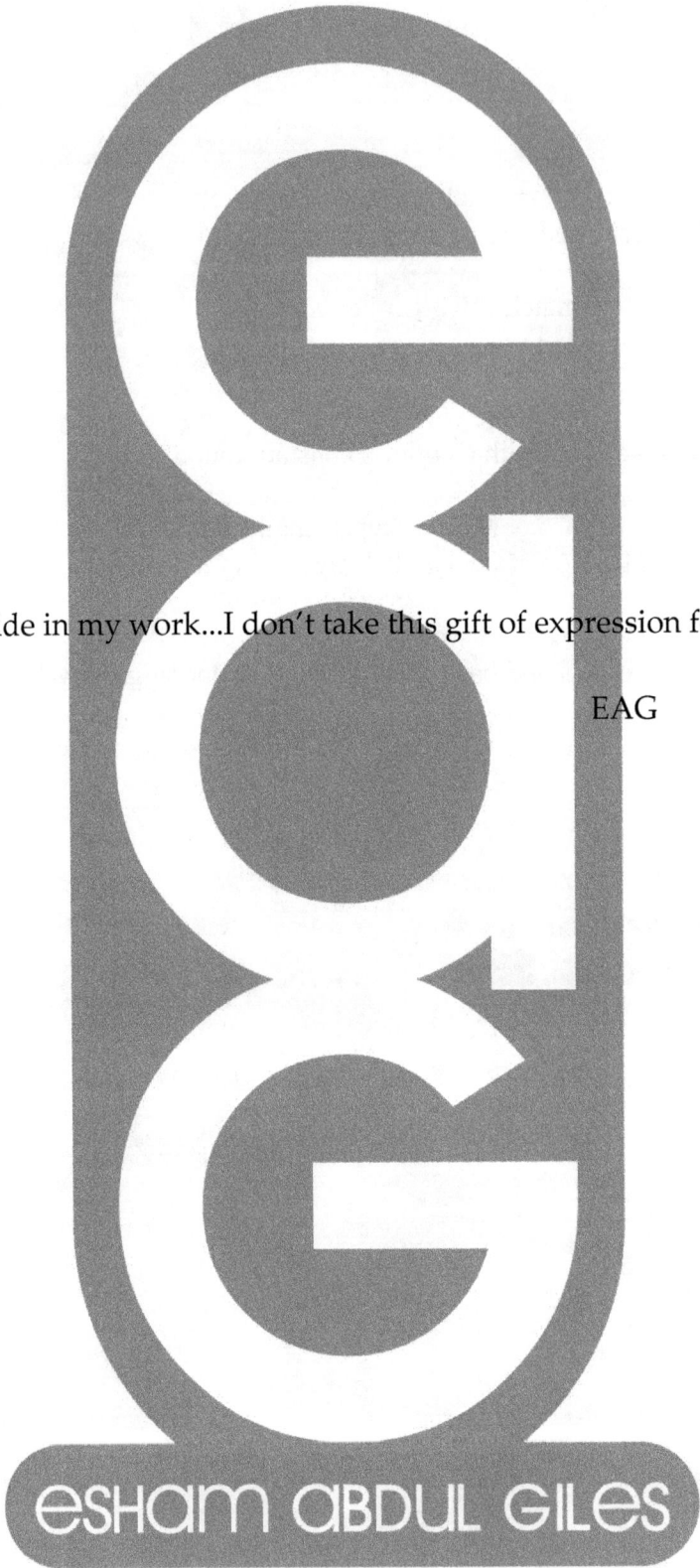

I take pride in my work...I don't take this gift of expression for granted.

EAG

ART OF SEDUCTION

I will seduce you and teach you a lesson,
Give full response to this like my man
Boogs, day of questions.
Smooth is the touch as the writing begins,
Like cocoa butter to skin,
Let me blend in.
Deep and romantic like Barry White,
Read this poem before you sleep at night.
Words on paper, thoughts coming on,
Like Marvin Gaye, "Let's get it on."
Splendid imagination,
I express so lovely,
I feel like R Kelly, "This writing's calling me."

You hear this voice, inside you,
The voice you've heard before.
Like Art of Noise, "Moments in love."
This voice has been there for you.
This voice has opened doors.
Arm grows tired constantly writing,
As I hand you this writing you are left in awe,
Like Billy Dee Williams, "Are you going to let my arm fall off?"
My writing is dignified and of careful thinking,
You tell me, "Esham, you're so good with the pen"
I say "thank you" like Denzel with the smooth cool grin.
My writing is the art of seduction.

esham abdul giles

If your attempts are futile, why continue to try?

EAG

eSHAM ABDUL GILES

SMS TEXT

Stop texting my phone!
I will never give you that chance!
Now you're all alone, mad because I'm not buying what you're selling.
Please come see me!
Absolutely not!
Now who's sad?

You text every other minute begging for me to listen,
You don't seem to understand English maybe you'll understand Italian,
"lasciarmi solo sciocco!"
Thanks Giusepp, some seem to never get it.

I'm like the cell phone folks, "Can you hear me now!"

No need to be sad or have a frown.
Why are you calling?
You are wasting your time.
I am telling you that it will be nothing.
You do not have the ability to change my mind.
Your efforts are futile.

Stop texting my phone!
I will never give you that chance!
Now you're all alone, mad because I'm not buying what you're selling.
Please come see me!
Absolutely Not!
Now, who's sad?

esham abdul giles

You saunter like a snake
your curves defined and
onyx skin like a panther,
a combination
without hesitation
most men
want
to
taste.

EAG

esham abdul giles

THE BEAST

Stalking through the dark of night,

Dressed in a short skirt and Manolo heels

She's giving them what they want to see.

She's curvaceous and sexy,

Slick and witty only in the party life she is cunning and has the power,

Seeking all which she'll devour.

Slipping in and out of shadow

Her hunger growing ever stronger.

Frantic now, in ravenous need

she scents the air for her prey.

Nothing she represents is true,

The beast will only bite if you let her get close to you.

Tame the cunning beast!!!

Stupidity and lustful fools walking into her path

Never knowing of the danger.

With speed and skill she lunges forth

Ripping, tearing at the dupes.

The next club, the next trick

esham abdul giles

The scene is always live and ripe
She's feeding on the endless nightlife.

THE BEAST

GAGA

esHam abdul Giles

Who says we can't imagine the perfect night?

EAG

esham abdul giles

Heels, Wine, Grapes, Cheese and Crackers.

Boy shorts, fitted camisole and heels.
He's looking at the Merlot as it chills.
She puts on a movie, "Jason's Lyric" to be exact.
He sits her near and holds her tight, Luther Van Dross playing low, "if only for one night..."

Light the candle, dim the lights
Your feet in those heels look so right.
Walk to the fridge and get the grapes.
Sure honey is there any other thing you would like to taste?
Absolutely lady, are you kidding me!
Bring out that nice platter of cheese and crackers.
Strut back over here, you feel me staring at cha.

Sit down let me take this all in,
Heels, wine, grapes, cheese and crackers
What's going through my mind you could only imagine.
Sip the wine, eat some cheese and crackers, and top it off with some grapes. I feel good, no, damn, "I feel great!"
Slight yawn my stomach is full like I just ate a full plate.
Sorry lady but we need to finish this at a later date you gave me too much food.

esham abdul giles

When I ask a question, nine times out of ten, I already know the answer.

EAG

esHam abDuL GiLes

QUESTIONS TO ANSWERS

Why did you come?
I was sent to you.
What is your purpose?
To lift you up when you're down.
Where are your friends?
I have no friends as I am trying to make you one.
What do you see in me?
I see pain, I see sorrow, I see a man who has a look in his eye as if there is no tomorrow.
I'm at a breaking point...how can you possibly keep me together?
I will be supportive and understanding.
Is there anything you think I should know?
No, I'm up front and everything will show.
Are you intimate with anyone?
No, I'm not; I haven't been in a while.
 I sleep alone. I'm in need of some down time.
Who do you sleep with?

esHam abDul GiLes

ANSWERS TO QUESTIONS

I spotted you coming out the Hilton.
Can I party with my friends?
You lied to me and I told you that I have zero tolerance for non sense
I told some of the truth; can you please give me a chance?
This is tainted and before it ever begun.
Why because I went out for a night of fun?
You should have been honest and just kept it real.
Can you please give me chance? I assure you this will heal.
Nothing means much to me anymore.
Why are you going?
I'm done before this has begun; your lust and night of fun has cost you this one.
Why are you going?
I don't know. I have never moved past betrayal.
Can we be friends?
Do not wait for me. I am tired and I want to be left alone.
How long shall I wait for you?
NEVER! That should answer your question.

QUESTIONS TO ANSWERS, ANSWERS TO QUESTIONS

esham abdul giles

"There are always rules to the game."

EAG

esham abdul giles

SHE WANTS ME TO BE HER SECONDARY

I've been dealt this hand,

So I play like a champion.

Does she understand the position she's in?

We go about our lives like nothing has happened.

The question is, "Why pretend?"

That you're really happy with the life you're in?

Because if you were you wouldn't constantly consider cheating on him.

If you made a commitment and you're obligated to stay,

Then why while he's away you want to play,

Breaking the light of day

Knowing all a long you cannot stay.

In my arms you feel more comfortable you say.

I'm like, "oh okay!" Looking at you sideways.

Knowing all along this cannot be,

She wants me to be her secondary.

But 1+1 doesn't equal 3.

How can you make the call on whose good enough for me?

esham abdul giles

You can't get mad if I decide to go out or date

You're not a victim here, starved for affection,

So why do we have beef or constant run-ins?

Don't you think that's something you should settle with your husband?

You really don't understand the position you're in,

This is a game no one can win.

I'm single; you're married,

You answer to him.

You have to end the old game before a new one can begin.

esham abdul giles

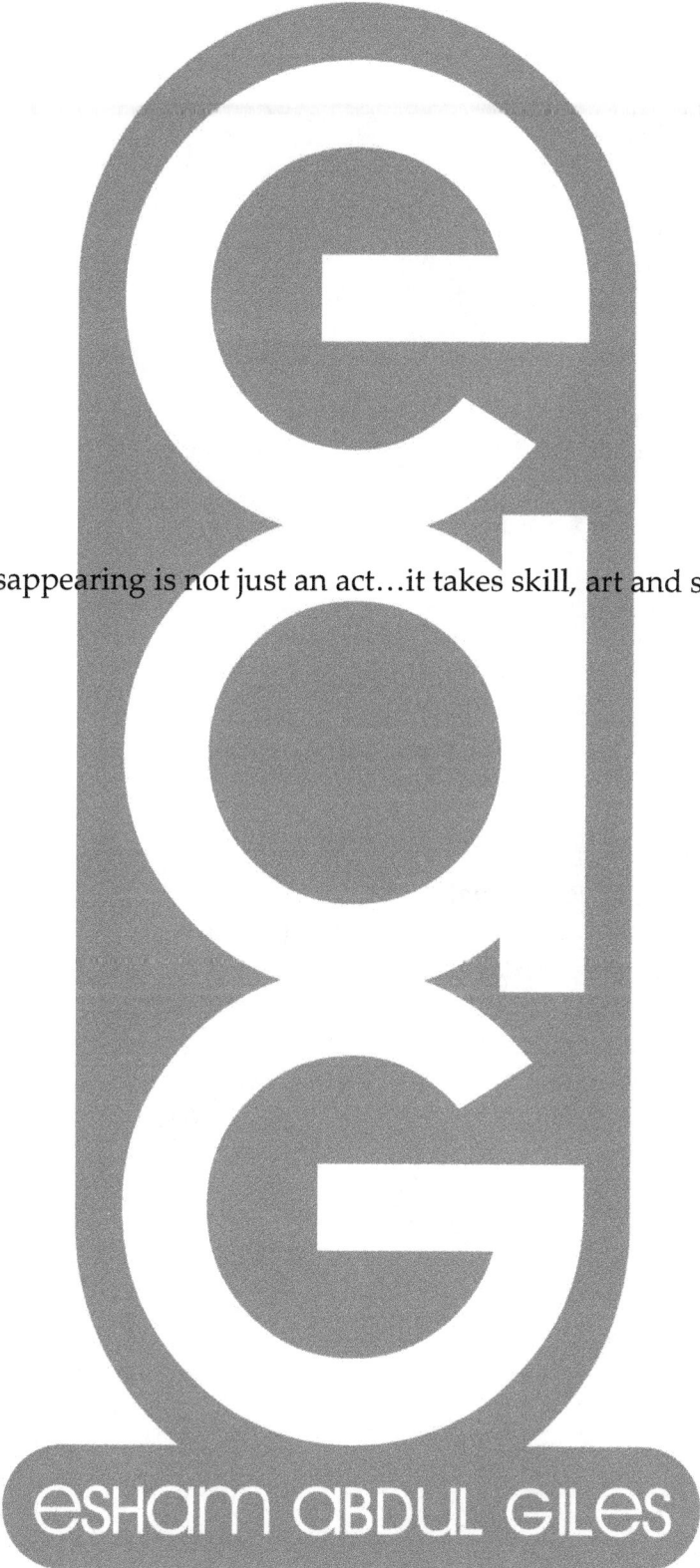

Disappearing is not just an act…it takes skill, art and smarts.

EAG

esham abdul giles

Houdini Machiavelli

Each escape
Involved some art,
Machiavelli smarts,
Houdini from the very start,
At least a brief
Incomprehensible
Exchange between
The man and the lady
during which the
Bond was sealed
Not broken
as he and she
blended. But the
end result
he had to
extract himself. It
was the hardest
part to get right
routinely breaking
away disappearing in dark of night.
Same as Houdini but with Machiavelli smarts (wink)
And as I so eloquently stated,
Each escape
Involved some art,
Machiavelli smarts,
Houdini from the very start,
at least a brief
Incomprehensible
exchange between
the man and the lady
during which the
bond was not broken.

esham abdul giles

"We will all be judged the same in the final hour...by our intentions and our actions."

EAG

DOUBLE STANDARDS

There's a saying, "a woman can't do what a man can do."
Although they try often to perfect being slick
In the end of it all they are labeled and look mighty ridiculous.
Although there are no rules to this game being played
Double standards are silent and they are here to stay.

She wants to play the game
Double up, Triple up
Holding down all these personalities at one time,
But her nature of emotion, feeling and deception won't combine.
Still, the man in this game can bob and weave
Stick and move, stick and move
Treating them all like numbers on a fast food menu.
She's with me; she's with him and him
Knowing that we are all close friends
Discussed at the party the myriad of compromising positions she has been put in.
He's with her, a friend, and a few of them
He's discussed the same way,
and curiosity leads the ones who haven't experienced his trickery his way.

Double Standards

Men feel no shame for being captain to this, the oldest game;
The dream job which many often proclaim, would be to make the grade,
For doing just 'what they do best'
And doing 'it better than the rest'
To pass 'staying power' is the test,
Oh yes! Oh yes!
Tell me you don't see the double standard in this.

esham abdul giles

"I cannot and will not change who I am to appease anyone."

EAG

THE LAST GENTLEMAN

He is and always will be a gentleman,
Sharp, confident, and serious.
He wears a modest smile.
His clothes are sure to be
In the latest style.

But what does that all truly mean?
Because he's more than just measured by appearance for what is seen.

The last gentleman,
abandoned to his fate.
Within this shallow world,
He has arrived too late.

The smooth talker abides here,
he who claims the day.
He wins the lady's heart
through wild and wicked ways.

The thrill of excitement
Will be her souvenir,
While her matchless beauty
Endears him to his peers.

The gentleman watches,
But cannot understand.
When he tries to save her,
She will not take his hand.

In her eyes He holds no excitement;
she tells him he's a bore.
She prefers the smooth talker,
Like those she's loved before.

So he sheds his class,
His grace and respect he locks away.

126

He dons a new mantle,
To help him win the day.

He sweeps her off her feet,
And the world starts to mourn.
As the gentleman dies,
A new smooth talker is born.

Now, the reversal as he bends to give what she asks for
Parties, clubs, flashing lights,
Every week opening up a new door.
Shallow minded statuette, He is totally bored.
He must return to the man he was before,

A gentleman.

The sun came up, his nightmarish dream was gone
It's memory, though, lingered on
Now he stands before you, honest and true,
he is who he is, and not because of you.

The Gentleman lives and he's praying for you.

esham abdul giles

The Prophet Muhammad (SAWS) stated, "Women are married for four reasons: For her wealth, for her lineage, for her beauty, or for her religion. So marry the religious one or you will lose."

Hadith narrated by Abee Hurayrah (RA)

esham abdul giles

WOMEN VS. WOMAN

She's covered from head to toe,
Masha'allah
Leaving nothing to show,
But her beautiful glows...GROWN WOMAN!
MODESTY, MODESTY, MODESTY!

She's not impressed or moved by crowds,
The further away she stands,
The more she stands out...GROWN WOMAN!

The Woman I admire wants to attain higher,
Howard, Rutgers, even community college,
Not worried about entertaining friends,
As she acquires the knowledge.

She wants us to be happy,
Protecting and guarding our foundation is top priority,
Husband and Wife, we grow our family... GROWN WOMAN!

The Woman I desire wants to build with me,
Not treat me as her personal cash machine.
Without malice or intent,
She has compassion and empathy.

The Woman I grow fond of,
Is grown in her speech,
Grown in her appearance,
ALHAMDULILLAH she's not needy or thriving for attention,
By has-beens, self-centered bigmouths with hidden agendas.

esham abdul giles

129

Religious not just in the word,
But in her actions,
Fearing the Hell's fire,
Worldly things never a distraction.

The Woman I ask for
is busy with ALLAH
not parties and drinking every
fifth hour...Such admirable power!
Subhan'Allah! Alhamdulillah! Allahu Akbar!

The Women I observe
Certainly deserves
Better respect than what she get's,
Love yourself; regain self-respect,
Stop putting yourself out there as an object.

The Woman I appreciate
Is much disciplined.
She's not perfect but she's learning from her mistakes,
Making her the greatest of all them.
Knowing all who she meets on her path aren't meant to travel a long her way.

But the Women I see, sad to say,
Most go about life in a backwards way,
With no thought or intent to sincerely pray.
Thus, living a life with no direction and
To be constantly treated in such profane ways
Though they are not made for this!

esham abdul giles

The Women I see think beauty
runs skin deep. Shallow!!!
It's not about looks.
It's about treating people equally and with respect
according to all Holy Books.

Bringing me back, to the Woman I know,
Who is advised to follow,
The Sunnah of our beloved Rasulullah, Seal of the Prophets,
Spiritual Growth....Spiritual Glow.

The Women I judge
without harm or harsh words,
often harbor a grudge
But the one who abuses her and takes her for granted she claims to love. Where is
the self love and self worth?

"Men are the protectors and maintainers of women, because Allah has made
one of them to excel the other... (Surah An Nisa, Ayat 34)"

The Women I hurt (by stating what's wrong)
Please do not consider it a curse but a gift.
It is better that I encourage us to build righteously together
Our families, ourselves, our love
because surely the Creator desires not backsliding but Uplift.

A WORTHY WIFE IS A CROWN FOR HER HUSBAND, BUT A
DISGRACEFUL WOMAN IS LIKE CANCER TO HIS BONES.
PROVERBS 12:4

For the WOMAN that I deserve and deserves me.

esham abdul giles

Chapter Six: Ego, Strength, and Power

So long as you have vision and the will to get things done, you will succeed.

EAG

esham abdul giles

SEAL THE DEAL

Let's seal this deal.

So much to talk about everybody listens,
These thoughts are burning my mind like nitroglycerin.
Some say I sound like a teacher when he gives a speech,
Can I express myself sincerely and directly like my man LaMeek?

Politics, War and all of this Poverty,
Give me a topic. I'll write about anything.
Can't sleep at night tossing and turning,
Brain on overload like caffeine and speed.
As I can only speak on things that's real,
The goal is to sign a multi book deal.

My mind is biblical quotes,
The lines I write are truly inspirational.
Like Rakim, "I ain't no joke!"
Auto focus, very amazing,
Like good money from insider trading.
My mind is a bully on beast mode,
You heard the man, "Here comes DEBO!"

esham abdul giles

133

I massacre these words as I overkill,

Don't make me Suge Knight this book deal.

Mind established in 1972,

Speak with caution,

Oz, Hamed Khan, I'll break you in two.

I give you the raw very sensationalized,

My words are neither scripted nor plagiarized.

Read one line as it captures the eye,

This dude is bad like Octavia Butler and Stokely Carmichael

Mind of the matrix, infinity, binary code,

Compute this knowledge as it's told.

Belligerent fools go ahead and rate this.

As a matter of fact tell me what the first State is.

People run mouth a mile a minute,

Buy the book then become the critic.

This is light hearted but the real can feel,

The ink is dry on this book deal.

esham abdul giles

We know that all systems of knowledge come from the Creator (SWT). We also know that most of the early understandings, literature, science, and art proliferated on the continent of Africa.

Anonymous

eag

esham abdul giles

MOUNT OLYMPUS

Meet me on Mount Olympus,

If you can get with this.

I drop knowledge like Socrates,

Thunder bolts like Zeus,

I go deep like Poseidon,

I am the truth.

The divine mind, I stay in all books,

Never limiting myself as you see by my work.

King of all Kings,

Children from Queens,

Aphrodite, my Princess,

And my Prince who will be King…Hercules.

Education and the ability to create by any means,

As fate would have it,

I am KING.

I drop knowledge like Socrates,

Thunder bolts like Zeus,

I go deep like Poseidon.

I've already jacked Imhotep,

Now my attention is focused on you,

Because if you can get with this

 bring your power to the business,

I sit and wait patiently for you to join me on Mount Olympus.

esham abdul giles

Swagger, " Either you have it, or you don't."

EAG

SWAGGER IS FOR BOYS CLASS IS FOR MEN

My swagger is confidence,

it's my humility, it's my ability

to carry on nonchalantly.

My swagger is definitely not something of the norm,

It's calm and dangerous, call it quiet storm.

My swagger can bring about peace to any confusion,

Smooth like Denzel, Training Day ruthless.

My swagger is not of arrogance as that has no place,

It's bowing out of a situation with absolute grace.

My swagger is not my clothes as I bring about a sense of style,

It's my humility that makes everyone smile.

My swagger is respect, it knows no conceit,

It's lifting you up when you're close to defeat.

My swagger is calm and definitely grown,

It's wanting to sit in a dim lounge all alone.

My swagger like Harlem renaissance it's influence has no end,

this my blessing of walking amongst men.

My swagger sharp without one ripple,

Like nice things but keep it simple.

My swagger is modest not up in your face,

It walks with all people equally.

My swagger is about pleasing myself not competing with the rest

It's my sharing and being selfless.

My swagger is alluring as I can persuade you with charm,

Get to know it, he means you no harm.

My swagger is my likeness; my gravitating aura,

It's also my patience and the ground I cover.

Swagger is not about material or high end jewelry,

It comes natural, it's a GOD given ability.

GOD

eSHam abDUL GILeS

A wise KING winnows out the wicked; he drives the threshing wheel over them.

PROVERBS 20:26

esham abdul giles

DISSECT THE KING PART ONE

Destroy, conquer and rip him apart
They constantly try to figure him out.
Where has he been, who is he with, is she his?
Break down the walls, we will destroy and dissect the KING.
Danger, danger the masses want to kill,
they lie; deceive, ultimately wanting his blood to spill.
There is no Astrologer who can search more deep in this than I,
The power to disappear right before your eyes.
Because he's reserved and low
He's nearly impossible to see just like a ghost.
Don't get it twisted, the KING is near
Make a call to fellow KING if he wants to go cheer.
Double R, Release the Double Blacks,
It's nothing, a regular thing when time to act.
I'm no pawn is what they say, so step off, be gone, speed on,
Before some BOSSES bring you just what you're asking for.

Kill the KING, Tear him down
Kill the KING, Strike him down
Dissect Him from Inside out.
Where's the young princess,
She's never seen? Is she his?
Is she protected by the KING?
Go on try and figure things out,
That's what peasants do, continuously run-off at the mouth.
Treason, treason, the spectator looms again, No honor only
Betrayal to bring about an end with the KING and a close friend.

Kill the KING, Tear him down
Kill the KING, Got to take his crown.
Destroy yourself trying to take the crown made of character and humility,
Prayers for you to let go of that devil and his envy.
Where's the Queen? Is it she who has spoken,
Is she the one whom the KING has chosen?
I give you nothing to figure out. Why make it easy,
That's why you remain peasants, you know everything.
Kill the KING Tear him down
Kill the KING Strike him down
Dissect Him from Inside out.

142

Love and faithfulness keep a KING safe; through love his throne is made secure.

PROVERBS 20:28

esham abdul giles

DISSECT THE KING PART TWO

My Skill goes beyond the depth of these one track minds;
All praises are due to ALLAH that I've grown to be very wise,
A grateful KING of these trying times.
By the end of all things from which I can tell,
ALLAH states that all things will be well...A peaceful place to dwell.
There is no Astrologer who can search more deep in this than I,
Dissect the KING they continuously try,
Give good reason why I should be vanquished from this earth?
You can't! That's what causes you so much hurt;
But all to no end, the times they will mend,
GOOD Men shall take place,
BAD Men silenced with Disgrace,
They'll know it was then but a shameful Strain,
To go against the KING without using their Brains,
I don't build on eras long since gone,
I build on just, all things come new,
Something I can call my own.
For sure by the end of all things, all will be well,
For ALLAH grants this KING a peaceful place to dwell.
My wisdom is not to be paralleled,
Most can't escape the bubble of vanity, they continuously FAIL.
Always calm as TRUTH comes to pass,
Dissecting has been reversed,
Quite the contrast.
The Lamb is now the Lion feed,
Quivering amongst the KING,
They walk in great Fear
I alone, am everywhere,
ENVIOUS tremble at the KING'S aura,
I grow large; they grow small, if any growth at all.
ALLAH'S Justice shall keep them in awe,
The KING quietly, calmly, ROARS.

Come challenge me if you're ready for WAR.
I sit in patiently in peace waiting for you to chisel me from the throne.

esham abdul giles

The KING'S heart is in the hand of the lord;
he directs it like a watercourse wherever he pleases.

PROVERBS 21:1

esham abdul giles

DISSECT THE KING PART THREE

The Final of three, come for me,
Your last chance to Dissect the KING
Our past, and present, fully express
All we could bear, all we have and would possess.
Wonder not that your forces could not bring
about destruction or demise of the KING.

Fate made by ALLAH with higher purpose in mind,
There's no KING by accident truly his Design.
Your HATE shall rule abroad, My Virtues are here.
The GREAT Conquest was denied,
I AM KING! Be gone with failed demise.
Don't think it strange that some so long have prayed for defeat
with one they claim to admire and love,
Selfish ways have got you here lonely dove.
Your Banishment of me which You Foes failed when designed
cloud your judgment and virtues, make mine brighter shine.
Option, Option, I analyze, research and study every single one,
I know fully when I invest the KING has WON!
Throughout your world of Gossip and grand illusion,
you know who's suffering and acting foolish.
Esteem caused you something evidently you didn't catch,
be careful not to envy, for this KING you are no match.
Subliminal and indirect, I see
I hear your hammer banging; driving the nail
You are no threat to me,
I'm prepared for the rain; I'm prepared for the hail.
KING Esham was taught very well.

There may be no end to this trilogy.
For I remain ultimately KING.

esham abdul giles

To truly be a star, you must shine in your light; create your own path.

EAG

These are the people who buy the life of this world at the price of the Hereafter;

their penalty shall not be lightened nor shall they be helped.

Qur'an Surah al- Baqara 286:86

Star WARS

Who told you not to be yourself?
Why would you want to be someone else?
Sports figures, Entertainers, Reality TV;
Everyone is a STAR but me.

My life is boring.
Nothing great to talk about,
While Basketball Wives has the ideas and fashion out.
I need to fit in, I'm loving them.
I love all the action and the games,
I do what I must to be a STAR by any means.

Trying to be someone else and not yourself comes with a price,
No Star was born over night,
Stay patient and true to yourself,
You will get your time to shine in the light.
Again, you have to trust and believe
YOU are more than someone else's copy.

Who told you not to be yourself?
Why would you want to be someone else?

Every celeb is on top of the world can't you see?
Everyone is a STAR but me.
Why shouldn't I become like Diddy?

No celebrity happened over night,
You are unique and a STAR born into GOD'S light.
You have purpose and GOD given ability,
Use it and see just how much you are a celebrity.
Soul search deep; no need to look far,
Master your own ideals,
no more struggle with Star WARS.

esham abdul Giles

148

Black males in the USA face far more dire situations than what is being portrayed by the popular media: rampant unemployment, senseless self deprecation and violence and failing education statistics.   We can't ignore that black males don't get the income and equality they should in America.

esham abdul giles

Black MALE

Are we destined to fail?
End up in jail,
Or only live long enough to be killed.
Extinction, inevitability, destined to be?
Please tell me what went wrong?
Are we to carry on until we're all gone?

Struggles and demons carried out generation after generation.
In general without proper upbringing and lack of love,
Can we find our place in this world of poison?

1960's and 70's the battle of the Heroin fiend,
80's teens caught in between,
90's gangstas, red versus blue coast to coast
Today direction of our Black Males lost as I've seen.

I have to question,
Are we destined to fail?
End up in jail,
Or live long enough to be killed.

Black on Black crime,
Dropping names to a broken system at the drop of a dime,
Black on Black hate,
No one wants anyone else to shine or escalate.
This needs to stop; it's never too late.

Because we aren't all destined to fail,
End up in jail,
Or live long enough to be killed.
Look at me I write freely,
Not behind closed bars,
Or hidden scars,
That's not your destiny.
We are Teachers, Mayors, Senators and Congressmen,
Doctors, Lawyers and UNITED STATES PRESIDENT.
Don't believe in propaganda that you are meant to fail,
You can and will be a successful Black MALE!

osham abdul giles

150

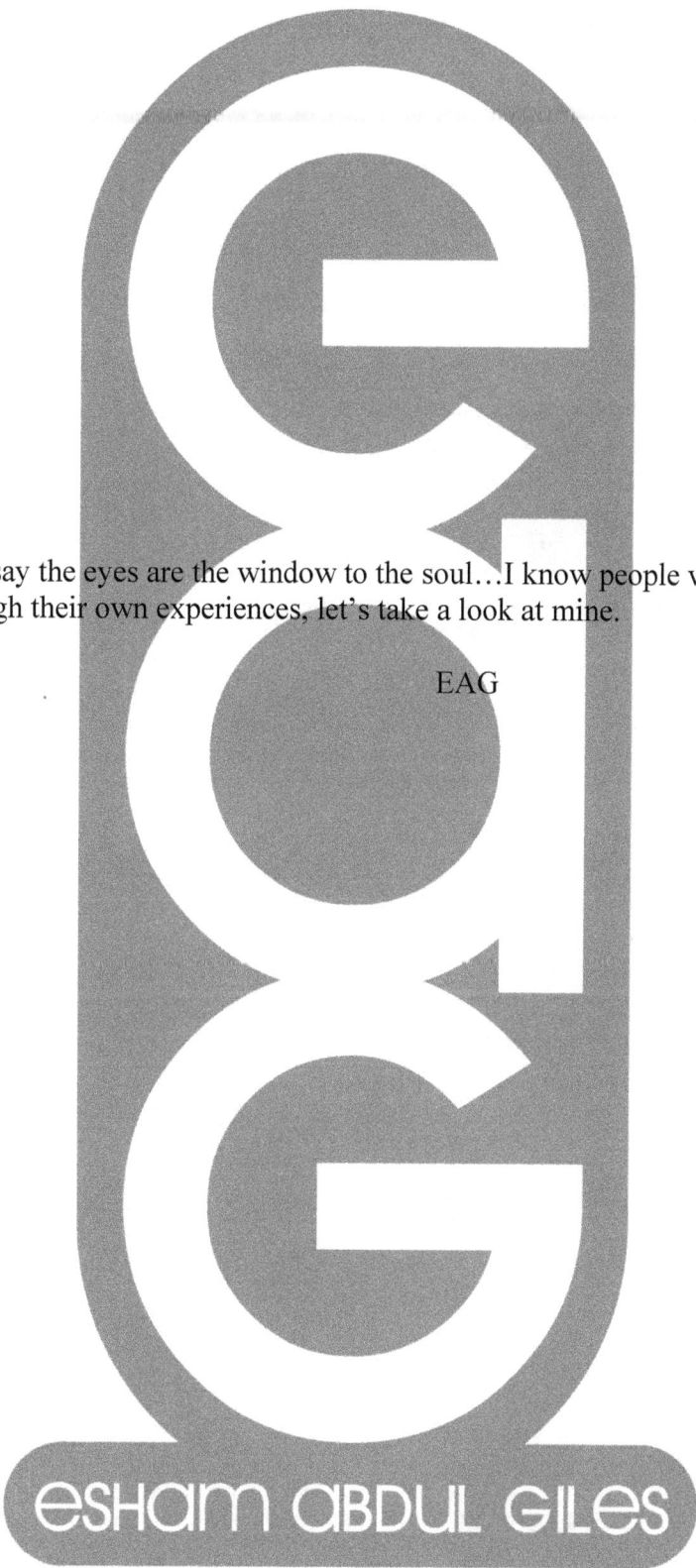

They often say the eyes are the window to the soul…I know people view the world through their own experiences, let's take a look at mine.

EAG

esHAM ABDUL GILeS

I´ll show you the world thru my eyes.

My Eyes show happiness my eyes show pain,

My eyes show strength my eyes seen blood stains.

My eyes show failure my eyes show growth,

My eyes show sorrow my eyes see hope.

My eyes show progress my eyes show hesitation,

My eyes show bleakness my eyes show there will be a destination.

My eyes show darkness my eyes show carelessness,

My eyes show forcefulness my eyes show fearlessness.

My eyes show focus my eyes show consideration,

My eyes show confidence my eyes show determination.

My eyes show that things aren't often clear,

My eyes show worries my eyes show I shed too many tears.

My eyes show calmness my eyes show faith,

My eyes show burning desire to be GREAT!

Look through the eyes of a man; you can see his soul.

esham abdul giles

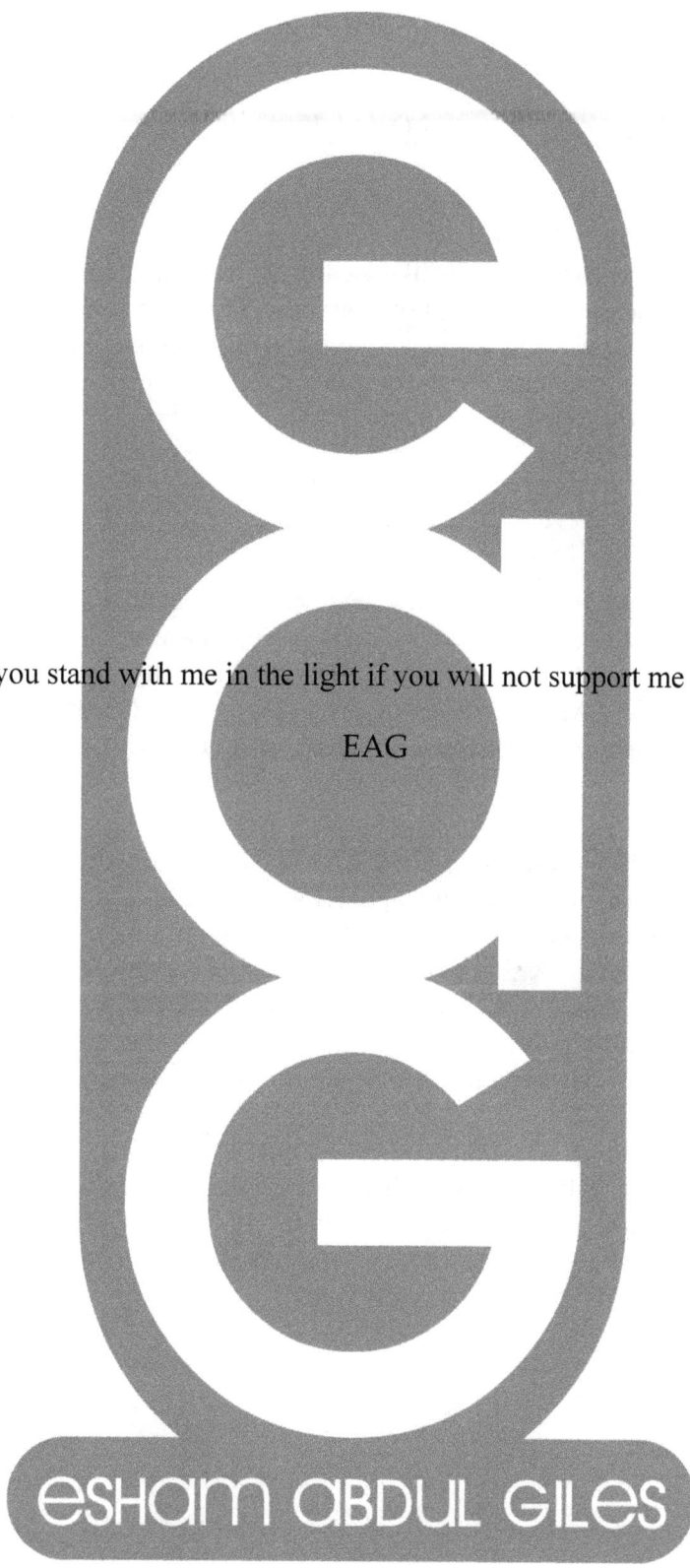

How can you stand with me in the light if you will not support me in the dark?

EAG

esham abdul giles

LOYALTY

Loyalty means being faithful to a person, it means to standby a person in all conditions. Regardless of prosperity or adversity, a friend is a friend. He or She transcends the petty worldly issues like wealth, power, and degree. Loyalty in a person shows he possesses integrity of character. These are some angelic qualities of man or woman. Loyalty. It's about friendship. It's about being there when someone needs you to listen...Needs you to witness their tears and keep their confidences... needs your help. Loyalty.

If you've ever had a crisis in your life, you'll know what I'm talking about. People you thought were your friends run for cover and disappear or worse, do the wrong thing and spread your misery as if it were the plague. Even worse than that is that when they have their own agenda and put that above loyalty. I understand that people make mistakes. Things are not always as they seem, but those are the times when loyalty counts even more. Loyalty. It's about friendship. It's about being there when someone needs you to listen...Needs you to witness their tears and keep their confidences... needs your help. Loyalty

I see the world in black and white. People you can count on, people you can't. I have a very difficult time seeing and appreciating the grays. Unfortunately, there is a very short list of people I truly know I can count on. I have friends that do not know that I am aware of what I would term as a massive betrayal of our friendship. I go on casually but know that I will never, ever, be able to trust them again. I spent the early part of life learning hard lessons and learning to read people quickly. I rely on perceptiveness and gut instinct more than anything people say or do.

Tell me you did the right thing when it counted, but if I happen to know differently, I will never trust you again. Loyalty. It's about friendship. It's about being there when someone needs you to listen...Needs you to witness their tears and keep their confidences...Needs your help. Loyalty

esham abdul giles

For He looks to the ends of the earth and sees everything under the heavens.

JOB 28:24

O mankind! We created you from a single (pair) of a male and a female, and made you into nations and tribes, that ye may know each other (not that ye may despise (each other). Verily the most honoured of you in the sight of Allah is (he who is) the most righteous of you. And Allah has full knowledge and is well acquainted (with all things).

Qur'an Surah al Hujraat 49:13

esham abdul giles

THE HOUSE OF WHO KNOWS WHAT AND PRESENT DAY FAKES.

I don't put down or blaspheme,

But time has come for me to call out these

Devote religious pretenders, posers, and fakers.

You talk about him, you talk about her,

You talk to and about each other,

Before leaving the House of who knows what.

Backbiting, slanderous hypocrites,

You people amuse me.

How can you sit there and claim to be blessed,

When you're continuously doing devilishment!

You fornicate, you commit adultery.

You pray these acts away, on your Sabbath day,

So your lust isn't revealed in the house of you know what…you FAKE!

The house is for repent and belief.

You can't possibly be truly listening.

We are to judge a person based on character,

As I am doing to you now.

esham abdul giles

Not a person's appearance or personal manner.

You are to repent not repeat those trifling behaviors that lead you away from Him.

You treat most like you won't answer for your errors because you are a member in good standing, ten percent tithing missionary from the house of who knows what

Routinely again and again.

 Sin after sin, come again!

On Friday offering Taubah, on Sunday testifying...

Nothing is sacred or holds meaning.

You will continue to do whatever it is that you do…this I'm sure.

But remember this when you walk from the doors of the house of who knows what

on to your eternal home

we will all have to account for everything

esham abdul giles

Surah Al Asr

103:1 By time,

103:2 Indeed, mankind is in loss,

103:3 Except for those who believed and done righteous deeds and advised each other to truth and advised each other to patience.

QUR'AN

ESHAM ABDUL GILES

TIME

Time is healthy, Time is ill,
Time will show enemies that have yet to be revealed.
Time moves forward, Time stands still,
If you don't put things into perspective, you can't climb that hill.

I make time to read and time to write,
My time to lead is definitely in sight.
Time is meditating as I constantly think,
Removing objects and immaterial things.
Time can be good and it can be bad,
Time is something some wish they had.

Time is useful; we tend to take it for granted,
Not realizing time can be gone in a New York minute.
Time can be long like soup lines,
Like Tupac said,
"You don't have to be in jail to be doing time."

Time is your past and is your present,
Learn from what was; make use of each second as this is a blessing.
Time is of listening and it's of difference,
What will you do when the time comes for your mission?

esham abdul giles

Believe me when I tell you this, "I'm not beat for anything…Never was, never will be."

EAG

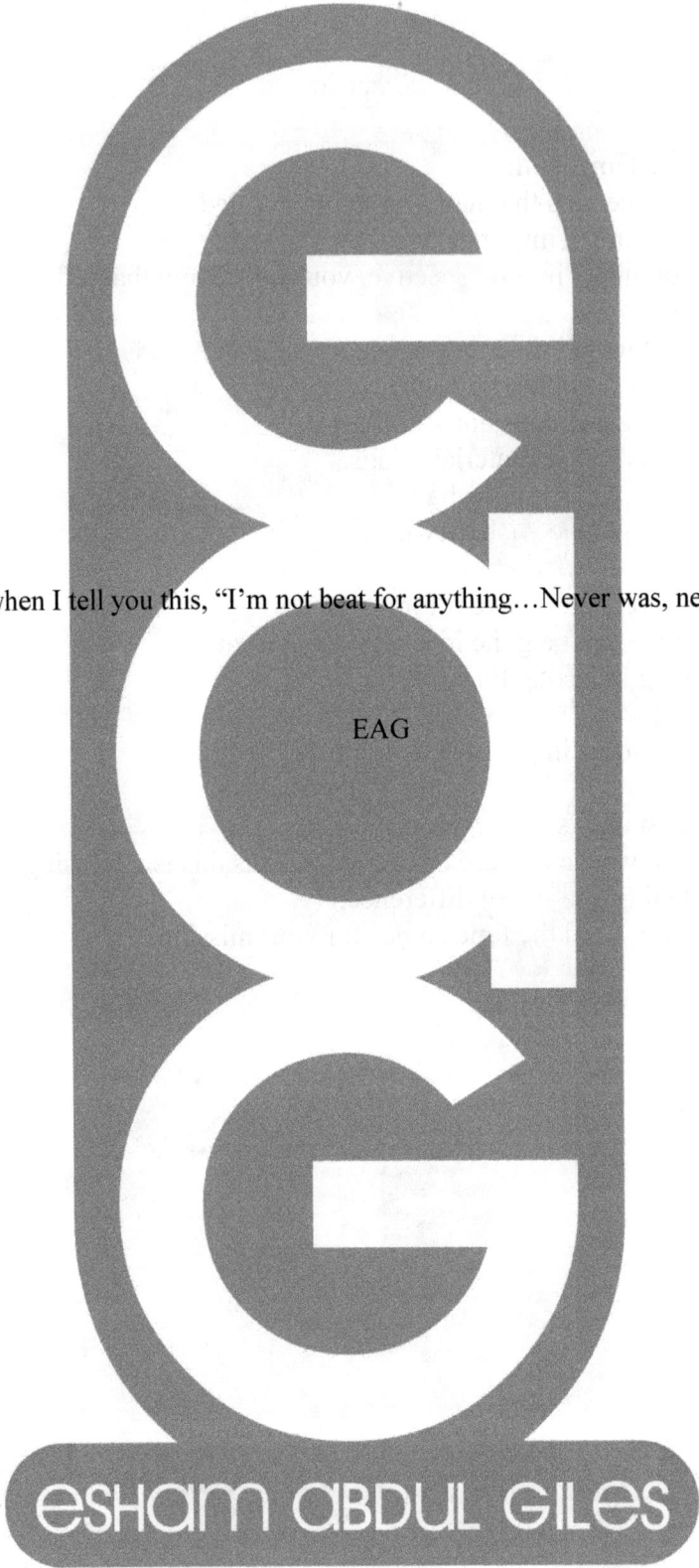

esham abdul giles

<u>FADED VISION</u>

The feeling of being watched, studied and judged was nerve wrecking,
The competition and petty challenges became predictable,
Made him realize things had to end for a new life to begin.
Doubt began to flood him. What he was planning?
What he was even now preparing to begin,
Surely Allah would see for He is the All Knowing.

FADED VISION

Is he corny; is he out of touch, Bars, parties, clubs?
He realizes he so done with what was.
He knows he's not better, that's never his position,
The noise and the crowds; the looks of inebriation...such a faded vision.
The rain; the ocean; quite time alone,
This is what he relishes as he is in his zone.

FADED VISION

Is he caught between Shaytan and the ocean of peace?
Surely Allah is the All Knowing he sees everything.
Is he at a standstill; a warp of some kind?
This can't possibly be, because he broadens his mind.
The lack of vision and progress from the world around him,
Makes him see different on who's really lost off in misguided direction.
Allah guides him keeps the wind behind him,
Stop the face of frustration as it shows over and over again,
I will grant you peace and redemption from this faded vision.

esham abdul giles

"Respect all men, regardless of what they may or may not have."

Vincent Giles

esham abdul giles

If you respect others, others will respect you.

JAPANESE PROVERB

Respect is not condescending; it does not put you down,

It's not trying to make someone look like a clown.

People respect a responsible person, who makes sound decisions, admits his mistakes,

tries his best in every situation.

Respect is the love for a friendship,

Respect is essential for lasting leadership.

It's easy to gain respect when you command it,

It's harder to gain respect when you demand it.

Respect is not thinking one is better than another, it doesn't try to

Deliberately hurt, if you don't have respect in the end you will be the jerk.

Respect is not cheating; it doesn't flaunt and celebrate sin,

It definitely doesn't sleep amongst friends.

Respect is to be given, to be received,

If you don't respect yourself you can't possibly respect me.

Respect doesn't yell, shout or bark,

It's about giving space when I don't want to talk.

esham abdul giles

Don't you think respect should have been taught at an early lesson?

Never mind, that's a rhetorical question.

Respect is value of others for this has been proven,

If you don't respect me, you will keep it moving.

Every human being, of whatever origin, of whatever situation, deserves respect.

esham abdul giles

"Esham, you can be anything in this world chose to be…you are my second oldest grand and I'm very proud of you."

Grandpa John Giles

IN THE COMPANY OF MEN

I'm savvy, I'm ambitious, and I'm keen,
But my ego almost cost me everything.
As I learn right from wrong, trial and error.
I never meant to cause no harm.
I never was big headed I come from modest roots,
My Grandfather constantly told me stay in my books.
As I learned, knowledge is a means, not an end, and today I stand in the company
of men.

This man puts forward, not because he wants to gain fame, he wants people to
learn from the mistakes he's made.
Decisions, so many things I held within.
Adversity, failure I was weary,
Allah! "What is my destiny?",
asking myself can he truly hear me.
The lying, the cheating, and degrading myself,
I was truly this man I blame no one else.
Life dealt me hard blows,
but I made the most of it,
as my walk has not come to an end,
I know I stand in the company of men.

But, this man is looked upon as a threat or danger,
why do they hate and hold so much anger?
People band together against him,
and have, oh! Such a majority on their side.
I'm not a bit worried I take it in stride;
the foolish don't know this won't bring about an end,
for I stride upright in the company of men.
As I move forward the cards are dealt,
I continuously learn more about myself.
I'm a man with vision, humility and precision,
I know that I'm here to carry out a mission.
My wisdom is a means, not an end,
This is why I stand in the company of men.

esham abdul giles

The believing men and women are protectors of one another, they enjoin the good and forbid the evil, they establish the prayer and pay the charity, and they obey Allah and his Messenger. They will be under the mercy of Allah. Verily, Allah is Mighty, Wise."

Qur'an, Surah at Taubah 9:71

O you who believe! Avoid much suspicion, indeed some suspicions are sins. And spy not neither backbite one another. Would one of you like to eat the flesh of his dead brother? You would hate it (so hate backbiting). And fear Allah. Verily, Allah is the One who accepts repentance, Most Merciful.

Qur'an Surah al Hujraat 49:12

ESHAM ABDUL GILES

167

FRIEND OF ME {"Frenemy"}

You hug, you smile

You say you even pray for me.

But deep down inside you and I both know you aren't what you claim to be.

I call you my peeps,

But you constantly deceive.

You say, "I'm your sister or I'm your brother."

But you go behind my back and sneak to be with my lover.

I remember you were there in my time of need,

You stood there with the knife and watch me bleed.

Don't know why some think we live in the land of make believe,

We know you are NO friend but our enemy.

You don't love yourself,

That's why you go about

Crossing, burning, and belittling everyone close to you.

To make yourself appear larger than what you really are,

A man or woman who was taught nothing as a child.

Competition is none as you claim to compete with me,

My aura is natural while yours is cosmetic, pathetic and lonely.

You scream for attention, "NOTICE ME! NOTICE ME!"

The problem is I did and held you in high regard.

I was the one true friend who cared about YOU not your image.

Still, I'll keep you close and truly pray for you,

Because in my case I'm an earnest friend who doesn't pretend to be.

You will see, as the ones you thought were real turn on you,
frenemy!

esham abdul giles

Chapter Eight: Clear Signs and Relief

Some experiences should be enjoyed and appreciated not questioned.

EAG

esham abdul giles

LAST SATURDAY A BUTTERFLY LANDED ON ME.

Last Saturday was a beautiful day,
A butterfly landed on me and decided to stay.
Is there truly a meaning of this scene?
Explain all three
Some say it's the soul,
Of someone we know,
Watching over us as we grow.
Some believe it's wisdom and everlasting knowledge,
In my case is this what she symbolizes?

Because last Saturday I was enjoying the beautiful day,
When a butterfly landed on me and decided to stay.
Some say she symbolizes rebirth after death,
Bringing about change and transition,
I'm in a good place,
I love my space,
She may simply symbolize the beauty of purity,
The Natural state.
Don't know why but it can be easy to speculate.

Because last Saturday on that beautiful day,
A butterfly landed and decided to stay.

esham abdul giles

I need a place where man has not influenced. With the beautiful natural landscapes all around me, my writing will never be dead.

EAG

esham abdul giles

Green Fields White Doves

Green Fields White doves,
Settling on a place I love.
Nature; beautiful, simplistic, serenity,
The dove resting upon the green field,
Peace all around me, "I love the way this feels."
For every moment of every spring and every summer
The benefit of what they bring: tranquility!
Harmonious sounds of nature enclose my surroundings,
Worldly things abandon; true purpose of living has found me.
Where serenity of the mind and purity of nature come together,
Green fields with white doves, the ultimate treasure.

esham abdul giles

Pray for what you want…your future can be brighter than your past.

EAG

And when My slaves ask you (O Muhammad SAWS) concerning Me, then (answer them), I am indeed near (to them by My Knowledge). I respond to the invocations of the supplicant when he calls on Me (without any mediator or intercessor). So let them obey Me and believe in Me, so that they may be led aright.

Qur'an, Surah al Baqara 2:186

esham abdul giles

AFTER THE RAIN, THERE WAS THE SUN

Betrayal, Abandonment, giving up on the ultimate
Shock and unbelief but you must embrace it.
Pull your arm back; keep your eye on the target.
Take a deep breath ignore the blood leading you into the darkness.
Take a step forward, don't dare go back.
Keep your hands steady, emotions in check.
Release your grip while eyes grow narrow.
You were hit in the heart with the cupid's arrow.
Keep moving forward, you won't get lost.
And continue on whatever the cost.
Tears will flow but you must fight.
The hands never go left, they only go right.
A brain with memories of the things said and done,
Can keep the heart bleeding, because you know that you have lost one. All you
can think of is the things that you regret; angry things that you have said. As they
continuously replay in your head.
Sorry and rain keeps you in your bed.
Don't sit and worry about how your love life fell to pieces,
It is what it is; Prayer and solitude should help you ease this.
Darkness can't last forever; open your blinds take a look outside,
I know when the heart is pierced nothing seems right,
But there is something out there that will make you smile.
Time heals all wounds; you will survive and win this,
Strong and vibrant you will look at love with bliss,
 Not a poker game betting with high risk.
We grow we learn; we learn we mature,
The next time love comes knocking open up your door,
Because, after the rain there is the Sun.
You are illuminated with brightness,
No need to look behind you.
Again you breathe and rise above
We all experience this in moments of love.

esham abdul giles

I can't live a life of mediocrity…I know there is something inside of me, pushing me to live a life filled with dignity, love, happiness, and pride.

EAG

eSHAM ABDUL GILES

THE FIRE

No one can know the potential,
Of a life that is committed to win;
The tragedies reveal a destiny filled with passion
With courage many challenges he faces,
To achieve great success in the end,
Is his burning testament.

There is inside of me
a burning flame
to be whatever I want to be,
all of the energy
to do whatever I want to do.
Promise to self, "remain true!"
I don't undermine my worth by comparing
myself with others.
If some were in my shoes would they even bother?

I carry the light of Lois Porter,
Five friends, as the past lives on to redeem the order.
And though at times it may seem too
difficult to continue to me,
I hold on to one thing, the FIRE!

I believe in the impossible,
hold tight to the incredible,
and live each day to its fullest potential.
I am the difference, never hesitate
And refuse to make the same mistakes.

So I, ESHAM ABDUL, possess the strength and the courage,
To conquer WHATEVER I choose,
It's the person WHO NEVER GETS STARTED,
That is destined FOREVER to lose!

The pain, The love, The lost, The life,
The eternal flame in my eyes, The FIRE!!!

THE BEGINNING

Bismillah Ar- Rahman Ar- Raheem
Al-hamdu lillahi Rabb il- 'alamin
Ar-Rahman Ar-Raheem
Maliki yawmi-d-Din
Iyaa-ka na'budu wa iyya-ka
Nasta'n
Ihdina-sirat al-mustaqim
Sirat al-ladhina an'amta 'alai-him
Ghair il-Maghdubi 'alai-him wa
La-d-dallin

In the name of Allah, the Most Beneficent, the Most Merciful.
Praise be to Allah, Lord of the Worlds:
The Most Beneficent, the Most Merciful:
Owner of the Day of Judgement.
Thee (alone) we worship; Thee (alone) was ask for help.
Show us the straight path:
The path of those whom Thou hast favoured; Not (the path) of those who earn Thine anger nor of those who go astray.

esham abdul giles

178

FOOTNOTES

Prolific definition found in Merriam-Webster Online Dictionary copyright © 2012 by Merriam-Webster, Incorporated

Paramount definition found in Merriam-Webster Online Dictionary copyright © 2012 by Merriam-Webster, Incorporated

Mighty definition found in Merriam-Webster Online Dictionary copyright © 2012 by Merriam-Webster, Incorporated

Eternal definition found in Merriam-Webster Online Dictionary copyright © 2012 by Merriam-Webster, Incorporated

esham abdul giles

esham abdul giles

180

esham abdul giles

esham abdul giles

esham abdul giles

esham abdul giles

184

www.ingramcontent.com/pod-product-compliance
Lightning Source LLC
Chambersburg PA
CBHW062100090426
42741CB00015B/3287